P9-APF-695

BOOKS BY LOUIS E. LOMAX:

THE RELUCTANT AFRICAN

THE NEGRO REVOLT

WHEN THE WORD IS GIVEN

THAILAND: THE WAR THAT IS, THE WAR THAT WILL BE

THAILAND:

THE WAR

THAT IS,

THE WAR

THAT WILL BE

THAILAND:

THE WAR THAT IS, THE WAR THAT WILL BE

LOUIS E. LOMAX

RANDOM HOUSE NEW YORK

Second Printing

 Published in New York by Random House, Inc., and simultaneously in Toronto, Canada, by Random House of Canada Limited.

Library of Congress Catalog Card Number: 67-25075

Manufactured in the United States of America
by The Colonial Press, Inc., Clinton, Massachusetts

Designed by Carl Weiss

To Robinette,
she kept the faith

INTRODUCTION

This book is more than an account of what I saw and heard while in Thailand. I have attempted here to put the Communist insurgency now raging in Siam in the context of the entire Southeast Asia crisis; most of all, it seemed imperative that the history of modern Thailand be compiled and rendered in a fashion comprehensible to the general reader. This task required massive research, and even then, could not have been accomplished had I not shared the trust and friendship of several Thai intellectuals who lived most of the history

I was researching. These pages were written with special indebtedness to:

- Professor Michael Moerman, The Thailand Institute, UCLA.
- Edward Turner, UCLA student and my library guide.
- Dr. Leo Rose and members of the staff of the Institute of International Studies, University of California at Berkeley.
- Sing Korn, my close friend and Thai guide. He saw to it that I met people and understood what they said. I, alone, am responsible for what I have written.
- The scores of people in Thailand who risked personal safety by sharing their experiences and views with me.
- Marshall Wright, Oscar Armstrong, and other members of the State Department who gave me all the help they could under the circumstances.

Then, there are these personal obligations: Billy Kirk helped me fly kites, helped me relax my mind when I had written myself into a corner. Robin Kirk always knotted the string and chewed bubble gum. She made me remember again the promise of youth uncluttered by a world of war and hate. Dorothy Hooper maintained both the house and her sanity while I plunged into a writer's funk.

Diane MacKay, Karen Kirk, Wynn Moore, and Marsha Kirk bore the impossible task of typing and proofreading this manuscript. Without them I simply would not have made it.

Most of all, I want to thank Ho Chi Minh, Premier of North Viet Nam. He invited me to visit his country and then slammed the door in my face when I reached Cambodia, five thousand miles from home. I went into Thailand instead. And that is where the action is.

It is no easy moment when a writer reads his own words and discovers that he stands against the policy of his government. It is even more disturbing when he discovers that he simply does not believe much of what his government has told him, much of what it has told others who also are trying to compile a document of modern history. Yet, the social critic must be honest with his generation. He must say the truth. How else are the people to know? And if the people do not deserve to know the truth, then they are not to be trusted as free men. I will always remember the woman who broke into tears during a lecture I gave in Minneapolis. Her only son had been killed in Viet Nam. Until she heard my talk she was unalterably convinced that Viet Nam consisted of two duly and freely elected governments, North and South; that North Viet Nam had attacked South Viet Nam; that the government of South Viet Nam had invoked the SEATO agreement and invited the United States to become its defense partner. What do you say to such a grieving human? Nothing. You can only pledge yourself to employ the small powers at your command in the hope that since man seems determined to die in wars, he will no longer die in ignorance. You can, then, write a book:

Thailand: The War That Is, The War That Will Be.

It is almost midnight, New Year's Eve. Merrymakers fill the streets, and the incessant din of car horns is punctuated only by the stacatto sound of fireworks. American soldiers on leave from the war in Viet Nam—men pathetically sad and totally drunk—stagger from bar to bar, from brothel to brothel. Members of the "American community" have gathered at an "embassy home" for the annual party; and high atop the Rajsubhamitra Hotel the employees of that establishment have gathered for their annual feast of sticky rice, spiced sauces, and pungent meats.

A festive air overlays the city; beneath the momentary joy, however, there is deep foreboding and nervous apprehension. Along Lan Luang Road, just around the great circle, American Baptists have gathered a group of well-scrubbed, middle-class Thai youths and they are singing "Jesus Wants Me For a Sunbeam." Two blocks further down the street, the Seventh-Day Adventists are telling the Thais that Jesus is coming soon.

But the great fear is that the Communists will get here first.

LOUIS E. LOMAX
Bangkok, Thailand
January 1, 1967

CONTENTS

Introduction

Appendix

THAILAND: THE WAR THAT IS, THE WAR THAT WILL BE

BURMA
MAE HONGSORI
CHIENG RAI
NORTH THAILAND
NAN
LAMPOON
SWANKALOKE
DAWNA RANGE
LAOS
PATHET LAO
RED CHINA
HANOI
THANH HOA
GULF OF TONKIN
NORTH VIET NAM
MEKONG RIVER
VIENTIANE
NONG KAI
SWANG DAEN DIN
NAKORNPANOM
SAKOLNAKORN
UDORN
PHUPAN RANGE
KOODTA KAI
BAN PAPARK
NAR KAE
KHON KAEN
NORTHEAST THAILAND
UBON
LAOS
PICHIT
CENTRAL THAILAND
CHAYAPOOM
TAKHLI
SUPANBURI
FREEDOM ROAD
BANGKOK
CAMBODIA
PURSAT
MEKONG RIVER
CHANTABURL
PHNOM PENH
SAIGON
SOUTH VIET NAM
BILAUKTAUNG RANGE
ISTHMUS OF KRA
ANDAMAN SEA
GULF OF SIAM
BANG BONG
THAILAND
PUNGAH
SOUTH THAILAND
SOUTH CHINA SEA
SADAO
YALA
ALOR STAR
BETONG
MALAYA

THE SEARCH FOR RASSAMEE

Shortly after noon on Thursday, January 5, 1967, a drab, clearly marked United States helicopter settled to a landing in an open field just west of the district military command post at Swang Daen Din, a Communist hot spot in northeast Thailand. The landing was a common occurrence, something of a daily carnival for the past several months. Laughing little children and their somewhat more pensive elders ran as one to the edge of the field and stood in a semicircle as the door of the helicopter popped open and the crew-cut, American pilot made the short hop to the ground. Then, far in the background and at the rear of the command post, a Thai barked an order and motioned his men forward with a wave of his machine gun. The heavily armed troops broke ranks; running like Michigan State halfbacks, they wove their way through the laughing, shouting crowd and scrambled aboard the aircraft.

"Tell them to get the hell off!" the startled pilot shouted, trying desperately to be heard above the chopping din of the whirling, overhead propeller. But the American's words fell on deaf ears: the Thai captain neither spoke nor understood English; the American pilot neither spoke nor understood Thai.

Flushing red from a mixture of frustration and anger, the pilot uttered an oath. "Look goddammit!" he shouted at the Thai captain, "this is what we are going to do today." Then the pilot knelt to the ground and unfurled a map of northeast Thailand. "These are the places we are going," he shouted, pounding his fist on the map. The Thai captain knelt beside him, unfurled his own map and began to pound and yell—in northeast dialect. And the children, their elders, clucking chickens, barking dogs, grunting pigs, and two silent water buffaloes, closed the circle to see and hear as the two shouting men all but beat their respective maps into the ground.

The yelling and misunderstanding mounted until a bilingual Thai—the hired interpreter of an American writer—clarified the situation: The pilot was under orders to fly twenty Thai soldiers to each of three danger zones in the jungles; he wanted the Thai captain to order his men aboard the helicopter twenty at a time.

"Then," the interpreter continued, "he will deliver those twenty where they must go and then come back for the next twenty; after that, the next twenty."

The American pilot and the Thai captain rose from the ground with smiles of understanding and relief on their faces; they bowed to each other politely. Within ten minutes the helicopter was airborne, carrying twenty men into the nearby mountain jungles to flush out the Communists.

The daily search for Rassamee, the twenty-two-year-old woman leader of the Communist guerrillas in that section of northeast Thailand, was on once again.

Treetops trembled mightily as the American craft made an almost vertical ascent and then veered out over the gaping, upturned faces in the marketplaces along Freedom Road, the dusty, American-built road that is the main street of Swang Daen Din.

"Bring her in or shoot her dead," an old woman shouted to the helicopter as she balled her gnarled fingers into a fist and shook it up as high as she could reach in the air. "That woman has caused us enough trouble."

The overwhelming majority of the Thai peoples would agree with the old woman, for the Communist insurgents have reduced both the northeast and southern tips of Thailand to enclaves of fear, plunder, and assassination; they have forced the one-time kingdom of Siam to invoke martial law and then go on to siphon off some of its best-trained men—a scarcity in Thailand—into the murky waters of counterinsurgency. More, Rassamee and her cohorts have caused the United States to irrevocably involve itself —men, money, equipment, and politics—in the internal war of yet another country in Southeast Asia.

However, understandably, many of the villagers of Swang Daen Din did not share the old woman's feelings. They simply stood silent, gazing into the sky as the aircraft climbed higher over their village and finally became lost in the sky over toward the jungle. For Swang Daen Din is Rassamee's town; many of the people there are her close relatives. Some of them, disturbing as the thought may be, are her followers.

The search for Rassamee (her name, in Thai, means "Ray of Light") encapsules the history and the magnitude of the Communist thrust that threatens Thailand. Born Rassamee Jandavongs,* in Swang Daen Din, she is the strikingly beautiful daughter of Krons Jandavongs, once one of Thailand's best-known intellectuals and an outspoken champion of the peasants in the northeast. A brilliant lawyer trained at Thamasat University in Bangkok, Jandavongs reached his greatest power fourteen years ago when the Thai government banned all activity of the Communist Party. The Thai Communists simply broke into smaller groups and continued to function under socialist banners. Jandavongs formed the socialist party in the northeast and took to the back villages, telling the peasant, and with precise truth, that his poverty was nothing short of immoral; he accused the government in Bangkok, again with accuracy, of regional snobbery and neglect. The central government became alarmed about Jandavongs' activity but was unable to curb him because Thai law at that time allowed freedom of political activity so long as one was not an avowed, open Communist. Then it came to the fore that Jandavongs, who had traveled widely in both Russia and Red China, was receiving money and munitions from China. Intelligence agents from Bangkok went on to claim that they had uncovered Jandavongs' plot to overthrow the central government and set up a Communist state.

One morning, in 1960, as the entire village looked on in horror, government troops marched Krons Jandavongs onto the very field where the helicopter had landed six years later and shot him to death.

The shot was quickly heard in Bangkok where Rassamee was finishing her third year at Thamasat Univer-

* It is all but impossible to translate Thai sounds into English. I have used simple phonetic renderings of these names to facilitate easy reading.

sity. A brilliant student, her childhood dream of following in her father's footsteps as a lawyer was not to be realized. Her father's blood was still wet on the ground when Rassamee vanished; she went first to Laos, then to Hanoi, to China, and finally to Moscow. Meanwhile the Communist apparatus in Thailand went underground, where it remains to this day. Close friends of Krons Jandavongs took over the leadership of his northeastern unit and stepped up their recruiting for the day Rassamee would return and bring her father's dream to fruition. Four years after her father's death Rassamee did return. Now a seasoned Communist and trained in guerrilla warfare, Rassamee quietly slipped into northeast Thailand (she came by night, by boat, from the Communist-controlled section of Laos) and assumed leadership of the guerrilla machinery.

Once the government discovered her activity it was too late. She had already gathered a force of men and pitched camp deep in the snake-infested jungles of the Phupan mountain range, which not only overlooks Swang Daen Din but curves through most of northeast Thailand as well.

Few people other than her followers and her victims have seen Rassamee since her return. She is on Thailand's Most Wanted Persons List, yet the combined efforts of the Thai and United States governments have been unable to unearth a single picture of her. But Rassamee's handiwork—burned bridges, murdered village officers and schoolteachers, stolen rice, and terrified villagers—is seen all too often, known all too well.

By midafternoon Swang Daen Din was a village of fright, surfaced over by the light gaiety of the marketplace. The villagers moved uneasily as they haggled and bartered for silks, scrawny chickens, and vegetables. The word was out: rice farmers from the back villages near the Phupan mountains had come into the district military office and reported guerrilla movements in the jungles. This meant that Rassamee was nearby, that yet another attack on Swang Daen Din was imminent. The orders of the sixty Thai soldiers who had been helicoptered into the jungle were simple: Find Rassamee and kill her before she eased into town by night and killed them. But even by day the villagers felt unsafe.

Fifty "home police guards," village men pressed into police service, patrolled the five hundred yards of Freedom Road that ran through Swang Daen Din. Garbed in khaki suits, military boots, and armed with American-made rifles, they walked leisurely along the dusty road, stopping to talk with friends, then pausing to eat glutinous rice and barbecued chicken at the Chinese-owned restaurant along the sidewalk.

The people are slow to talk to a stranger; after all, a stranger could be anybody—an agent of the Thai intelligence service in Bangkok, or a servant of Rassamee. And if the stranger is an American, then the chances are he could be an agent for the CIA. At first, even with the aid of my interpreter, I was unable to get villagers to talk about anything other than the weather and if Americans ate glutinous rice. We walked from market to market, from roadside café to roadside café; the response was always the same.

"The people are frightened," my interpreter Sing Korn told me. "Every time I asked one of them to talk to you about Rassamee, they told me to please go away and leave them alone."

Then a young policeman, a member of the home guard, walked up to our table. "I will talk to the American," he said as he pulled up a chair, sat down, and leaned his rifle against the table.

His name was Nai Dang (Mr. Red), and something was clearly bothering him. "They will never get Rassamee," Mr. Red said to me. "And if they do, there will be a dozen others to take her place. The situation is getting worse, not better."

Mr. Red paused long enough to mold a small cone of sticky rice between his fingers, dip it in the common bowl of sauce, and then continued.

"Those fellows in Bangkok are living in a dream world. They still don't take this thing seriously enough; they didn't take it seriously at all until you Americans got excited about it. But we have been living in fear of our lives for more than five years. Bangkok didn't care about us then; the people from the back villages were hungry, poor, and all but naked. They were neglected; all Bangkok did for them was to send in special police to arrest the villagers for gambling and brewing homemade whiskey. This is why so many young men have gone up in the mountains to join Rassamee."

I watched Mr. Red's pained face as he shoved the sticky rice into his mouth. "Have any of your friends joined Rassamee?"

"Yes," was the quick reply. "Several of my childhood friends are now up there in the mountains with Rassamee."

Just then, a huge United States Air Force truck, laden with supplies for the American airbase some sixty miles away, sped down Freedom Road, creating a blinding cloud of thick red dust that powdered our food and turned us into chalky gargoyles.

"That is what the fight is really about," Mr. Red said between coughs. "You Americans don't care about Thailand, about the Thai peoples—particularly those of us here in the northeast. All you care about is your damn airbases."

There was truth in what Mr. Red said. We had to supply our airbases from seaports in south Thailand; American engineers converted a bumpy and dangerous Thai road that ran from Bangkok to Udorn into a paved highway; then they widened an even more dangerous, dusty road that winds out of Udorn, through Swang Daen

Din and Sakolnakorn where it curves northward to Nakornpanom. Major American military installations are located at these junctions. The network of roads connecting them is called Freedom Road, or Friendship Highway.

"We must go now," my Thai interpreter said to me. It was late afternoon; even before we left Bangkok, Sing Korn made it clear to me that under no circumstances would we spend the night in a village near Freedom Road, for these villages were dangerous. These were his people. Like Rassamee, he was born in the northeast and then migrated to Bangkok in search of better employment. Now he no longer knew who among his people could be trusted. As a Thai, Sing Korn faced more danger than I. The guerrillas have made a point of not attacking Americans. But Sing Korn, now an unknown quantity among the peoples of the area, faced grave danger.

Freedom Road sloped southeastward toward Sakolnakorn and was jammed with military traffic. Overhead, American helicopters chopped through the air, ferrying Thai soldiers into the jungles. Even higher overhead, American jets roared and whined as they returned from their missions over North Viet Nam. Fog-thick red dust hovered over the two-way, single-lane highway; each time my driver moved into the left lane to pass a slow-moving car it was if we were driving into oblivion. It was impossible to see more than a few yards ahead; only a series of near miracles kept us from slamming into oncoming vehicles. But there was no alternative: the driver, Sing Korn, and I were afraid that nightfall would find us on Freedom Road, at the mercy of the Communists who frequently come down from the mountains to burn bridges, to rob, to kill. People simply don't travel the roads of northeast Thailand at night; for, as a local saying puts it, "If the Communists don't get you, the bandits will."

I was living in the world of the future, yet it was very

real and immediate. Freedom Road is the battlefield of the war that will be. Sing Korn, my interpreter, put it into focus for me:

"One day Rassamee and her men will cut off this road. They will burn out the bridges. Then you Americans will be in one hell of a mess; how are you going to supply your airbases then? What will happen when the Communists attack one of your airbases here in the northeast?"

Sing Korn raised an issue that American and Thai officials have long since resolved. At the moment—as we were doing in Viet Nam five years ago—the United States is working with the Thai military in an "advisory" capacity. We are training Thai intelligence officers and we are helicoptering Thai soldiers into the jungles to fight the Communists. But our pilots are unarmed; they are instructed to land the Thai soldiers several miles from the area of suspected Communist camps and let the Thais make it on foot from there. We are also training Thai pilots to take over the helicopter operation.

This is an excellent temporary face-saving operation for both the Thai and American governments. The Thais are proud and sensitive peoples. Bangkok is determined to prove that it can end the Communist insurgency without direct American intervention. America, on the other hand, is preoccupied with its airbases; we bomb North Viet Nam from Udorn, Sakolnakorn and Nakornpanom. We send helicopters aloft from Nakornpanom to rescue our downed pilots in North Viet Nam. More, these are the bases from which we will bomb Red China—some two hundred miles away—should that hellish day ever come upon mankind.

But if Rassamee and her followers commit a serious act —such as interrupting Freedom Road—then American men will take up arms and go into the jungles of northeast Thailand to kill, to die, in search of the Communists.

Both the Americans and the Thai Communists are playing a convenient waiting game. The current arrangement allows the United States to carry out its attacks on Viet Nam from Thailand, to assist the Thai government in the fight against the insurgents, without spilling American blood in the jungles of Thailand. Thus the United States can say—as it did once upon a time about Viet Nam—that we are not directly involved. The Thai Communists like it this way too; for the current situation allows them to play cat-and-mouse guerrilla warfare with the Thai government, knowing full well that the power of American arms and men will not be brought to bear. It is a nice, little, clean, deadly game: the Communists in northeast Thailand terrorize and kill only their fellow Thais; not a single American Peace Corps worker or United States Information Service officer—and they work in the back villages—has been touched.

The day of confrontation will come, of course. It will come when the Thai Communists feel they are strong enough, that the time is ripe. There is a view, and I share it, that the confrontation between the United States and the Thai Communists will come soon, on orders from Hanoi or Peking, perhaps both.

"One grave danger about escalating the war in Viet Nam," an American diplomat explained to me, "is that Hanoi may well order the Thai Communists to interrupt Freedom Road and kill Americans. Then we would have to go after them with guns and napalm. We would then be involved in two wars in Southeast Asia. And the hawks would get hawkier, the doves would get dovier; I don't know if the American fabric could withstand such a strain."

The experience was unnerving. I gazed out the window of the speeding car; there, in plain sight, and less than twenty miles away, was the guerrilla-infested Phupan mountain range. We know a good deal about what is going on up there in the jungles; but what we know is only a small portion of the whole truth. Nobody knows how many Thais are involved in the insurgency; we know who most of the major leaders are, but we know little about their followers. We do not have complete information about the sources of their arms, nor do we have the full facts of their financing. Then there is the question of communications between Rassamee and the leaders in other sections of northeast Thailand. Is it accidental that they ofttimes seem to act in concert? But the most disturbing question is this: How much support do the insurgents have from ordinary Thai citizens—from farmers, some of whom plant rice by day and become raiders by night; from businessmen, some of whom funnel a good portion of their profits into the insurgency coffers?

I have examined documents and equipment captured by the Thai government during raids on the camps—some twenty-five hundred insurgents either surrendered or were captured last year. From interviews with some of these prisoners a sketchy composite of life inside their camps can be made.

The insurgents are organized into bands of about twenty persons. They live deep in the jungles of the mountains; they sleep on the ground under plastic tents. The camps are protected by a network of wooden cowbells strung along bushes about a hundred yards from the center of each operation. Once a government soldier brushes against these bushes an ungodly racket is set off, alerting the camp. The insurgents are armed with a mixture of weapons, from crude bows and arrows, French rifles left over from the Indo-China conflict, to American machine guns captured in Viet Nam, as well as guns made in China, in Russia, and in Czechoslovakia.

The leaders were trained in Communist countries. They returned to Thailand and set up the organizational structure, with the old Communist Party as a base. Their hard-core line is that the "American Imperialists" have taken over Thailand, that the American government is supporting the Thai government in its political and economic tyranny over the masses, particularly in the northeast. The ploy has worked: thousands of young Thais, men and women, have taken to the hills to join the insurgents.

There is a steady flow of money into their camps from Hanoi, Peking, and from the Communist underground in Thailand. The insurgents keep meticulous books; runners are dispatched into small villages to buy supplies and every purchase is itemized. The big items are transistor radios, batteries, and dogs. These captured expense accounts tell volumes:

Much of their time is spent listening to anti-Thai government diatribes from Radio Hanoi (three hours a day) and Radio Peking (seven hours each week). The purchase of dogs indicates that Vietnamese are involved; Vietnamese eat dogs, Thais don't.

By day the young recruits are given courses in Marxism, Maoism, and guerrilla warfare. Their textbooks are simple tablets written in Thai by hand. They live mainly on rice stolen from or given by terrorized farmers. They are supplied by helicopters from the Pathet Lao in northern Laos, some fifty miles away.*

By night the insurgents pour down from the mountains into sleeping villages. They rouse the villagers, set up loudspeakers, and at gunpoint, subject the peasants to a long lecture (in some instances for four hours) on the glories of Communism and the evils of the government in Bangkok. Then they pass out application forms for membership in the Communist Party (usually disguised as "The Farmers Progressive Union"). Immediate converts are taken to the camp in the jungles for training. Each farmer is asked, again at gunpoint, to contribute

* Early in July 1967 the Thai government claimed it had irrefutable evidence that "Hanoi [was shipping] tons of supplies and men" to the insurgents by helicopter.

rice. If he doesn't have the rice on hand, he is ordered to have it gathered by the next full moon and told that somebody will be there to collect it.

As dusk fell, the Phupan mountain range faded from view. Even then, the American helicopters, their lights blinking, were still circling over the jungles. The Thai-American operation for that day had been futile.

Sakolnakorn is situated in the center of the insurgency danger zone. Yet it is known as a "secure town." One only has to walk the streets after twilight to understand why. The town is literally occupied by the American military. Soldiers jam the sidewalks; huge American military trucks clog the streets.

"Hey, man," a Negro soldier shouted at me as I walked into a sidewalk café, "you Army?"

"No. I'm a writer," I shouted back, trying to be heard over the blare of Thai music coming from the theater next-door.

"Well, write this," he ordered me as he cuddled his Thai girl friend. "I am not going back home if I can help it. To hell with Alabama! I've got a better go in the army; and that's where I'm going to stay. Man, I'm going to re-enlist until they run out of forms. I plan to stay right here with my baby. Ain't that right, mama?" he asked of her.

The Thai girl's brown face broke into a smile of agreement. "You number one," she replied in English that was all but unintelligible. Clearly, the Thai girl had not understood a word the soldier had said.

"That's right," the Negro rejoiced. "Big Bill from Alabama is *Number One*."

Big Bill's fellow soldier, a young white man from Virginia, leaned across the table and joined in the laughter. He too had a brown-skinned Thai girl friend. "We all might stay here in Thailand," he told Big Bill, "but not for the reason you think. If these Thai flyboys don't hurry up and wipe out the Commies, we will have to do the job."

"Man, I don't want to talk about fighting," the Negro told his friend. Then he turned to the waiter. "Hey boy," he shouted, "we need more beer."

Not all of the Americans in Sakolnakorn had come to make war against the insurgents and the Viet Cong. Some of them had come out of idealism, with the hope that American humanitarianism could save Thailand. I had just arranged for a table in the outdoor café when two American youngsters, a boy and a girl, came over to say "hello." They looked like denizens of Sunset Strip. She was in the Peace Corps, he was a community development worker. After the third beer, he began to brood:

"I am a veterinarian, you know. I have to work with the Thai community development director. Well, the cows in the villages need to be innoculated, you know. Like, that way I help build a bridge between the villagers and this Thai mother who has been pissing on these peasants for years, man. Like, you know, I could get the job done; but this Thai cat sits behind his desk on his ass and shuffles papers and signs documents. Meanwhile, man, the cows are giving bad milk and the babies are dying, you know. Like man, shit, you know, this Thai is something from way deep inside Bangkok. They must have an enclave where they breed these mothers. Like, we go in a village twenty miles from the main road. All the cows need innoculating, you know. Well man, like, that would take several days. But this Thai picks up and hauls ass out of there as soon as the sun begins to arch over the trees. He is afraid to be in the villages at night. The Commies might show. Well, hell man, you know, if you are afraid of the Communists, how in the hell are you going to urge the villagers to stand up against them? Like, I will stay in the villages and innoculate the cows. Rassamee can go screw herself. But the American government makes me work under this Thai cat. So when the sun begins to set, I have to haul ass when he does. You know."

Well, I didn't know, but I was rapidly beginning to understand. The American boy and girl buttoned their dirty trench coats, said "so long," and walked arm in arm into the chilly night.

The music was still blaring from the theater adjacent to the café. But from the sky the sound of circling helicopters was unmistakable.

The search for Rassamee was still on.

RASSAMEE IS NOT ALONE

The following morning I left Freedom Road and drove south to the village of Na Kae, an area that had recently been terrorized by the Communist insurgents. It was midmorning, but the shops were deserted, the marketplace all but asleep. A few villagers moved about on their bicycles eying each other, and strangers, with suspicion. One could literally feel the fear in the air. And the fear was more than justified; for seven weeks before, in November 1966, the Communist insurgents had come down from the Phupan mountain range and assassinated a village leader.

Built high on stilts and brimming with activity, the police headquarters at Na Kae was a heavily fortified fortress in the center of the ghost town. It was surrounded by barbed wire; inside the compound, sandbags were stacked four feet high. And behind the sandbags, some fifty home policemen, armed with large rifles and bayonets, stood on the alert. As Sing Korn and I drove into the compound some of the men actually dropped their guns and ran.

I asked to speak with the chief of police, only to discover that both he and his second in command were in the jungles searching for the Communists. But the third officer in command, Vicharn Tanapanick, a slight man in his late twenties, agreed to be interviewed.

"Last November," he said in halting English, "The Communists come into our village. They kill our spy. Then they talk about Karl Marx, take our rice and leave, back to the jungles."

"Were any of the Communists killed?" I asked.

"No, we did not kill any of the Communists. There were about twenty-five of him, but we did not kill any of him."

Inside the station twenty young Thai men were being photographed and fingerprinted. "We now have a local law," the officer in charge explained to me, "that every man in the village must be photographed and fingerprinted. He must carry his identification with him at all times. The law allows us to stop and question all males," he continued. "If we find a fellow without identification, we arrest him on suspicion that he is a Communist insurgent."

"Do the insurgents come down from the hills during the day and walk the streets?" I asked.

"Indeed they do," he replied. "They are regular Thai

citizens like everybody else. Some of them live and work here in the village; they become insurgents at night. We don't know who they are; we never know them until they strike."

"But what would keep a Communist from coming here and being photographed? It seems to me it would be a perfect cover to get an identification card and then be able to move around freely," I suggested.

"You are quite right," the officer admitted. "Many of them do just that. We know the law does not stop them; but we must do something. We can't just sit here and wait for them to kill us!"

A Chinese restaurant owner spoke for the villagers of Na Kae. "The Communists struck at night and most of the police ran like hell. They are all huddled over there behind those sandbags," he said, pointing, "but if you were to set off a firecracker there would be a wild stampede for the rice fields. We don't know from one day to the next if we will live or die."

Rassamee was not responsible for the terror that gripped Na Kae. Rather, the search in this section of the northeast is for one Yod Phathisawata, the fifty-two-year-old leader of the insurgents ensconced in the mountain jungles some one hundred miles from Swang Daen Din. Like Rassamee, Phathisawata holds a high place on Thailand's Most Wanted Persons List; the only available picture of him was taken twenty-four years ago, when he was twenty-eight. The "wanted" poster describes him as "tall, stout, white and broad-headed. He is one hundred and seventy centimeters high and he gets tattoo on his shoulders."

But a good deal more is known about Phathisawata. He was born about twenty miles from Bangkok and his name means "Luck in the Best Direction." He became affiliated with the Communist and socialist movements early in his life and migrated to the northeast where the Communists made much of the poverty and neglect in that area. Then came a strange development: Yod traveled to Laos where, for five years, he was a Buddhist monk. There is some evidence that even while he was a monk he was active in the Laotian Communist Party. He left the priesthood and traveled to Red China. He remained in Peking three years, and in 1964, returned to Thailand where he took over the underground Communist activities near Na Kae and organized his insurgents.

However, the Communist underground is not the sole underpinning of Phathisawata's carefully structured insurgency. Taking a page from the early history of Thailand, from the days when the king in Bangkok insured loyalty from the remote villages by marrying the fairest young maid in each community, Yod has taken unto himself several (some say as many as ten) wives from numerous remote villages in the northeast. One or two of these wives are reported to be with Yod in the jungles, but most of them are back in their home villages where they serve as excellent recruiters and as a source of rice and other staples as well.

The full impact of this conquest-by-marriage technique is realized only after one recalls the structure and nature of village life in Thailand. The back villages are extremely small—composed of, say, twenty-five families. The people live from the earth; their only contact with the outside world is by foot and transistor radio. The average peasant farmer has to walk, heavily burdened, to get his produce to the market in, say, Swang Daen Din or Na Kae. He certainly has few, if any, ties to Bangkok, eight hundred miles away. Within the village itself, the headman, himself a peasant farmer, represents whatever law and order there is. There are no police; rather, codes of conduct are enforced by tribal folkways. The villagers amuse themselves by gambling, and drinking homemade whiskey. And when police do come into villages, they come to arrest the gamblers and the bootleggers.

Michael Moerman, Professor of Anthropology at UCLA, and his wife, Marianne, spent the better part of two years studying life in the back villages of northeast Thailand. This is his description of his village:

". . . [It] is isolated, with no running water, no paved roads. During the rainy season only a single strand of telegraph wire [to the district office] or any unusually strong desire to travel connects [the village] to the remainder of Thailand. In the village, it is rare for anyone to receive mail. Not until 1960 did anyone in our village own a radio. The older villagers are aware only vaguely of the Thai nation; they know still less of any Western country. When we left," he concluded, "one old man with whom we often exchanged visits, still thought we came not from America, of which he had never heard, but from Ceylon, the land of the Buddhist scriptures."

The villagers into whose families Phathisawata has married are apolitical; their loyalties are to their villages and they have no concept whatsoever of the economic and political factors involved in the struggle between the Communists and the government in Bangkok. And what little the villagers do know about Bangkok, they don't like. The Communists, on the other hand, are from the Thai earth and the back-village rice fields. True, the insurgents carry out a campaign of terror and thus incur both the fear and the wrath of many villagers; but it must be noted that the terror is directed against the representatives of Bangkok—the schoolteachers, the police, and other government officials. All of the village headmen who have been assassinated have been in open league with Bangkok. The Communist approach to the villagers themselves is to promise that all of the hurts and pains of back-village life will be eliminated. Strange things result from these promises.

Prasort Vetimong, the son of a poor peasant farmer, was seventeen years old when one of the men of the village introduced him to a stranger. The stranger asked if Prasort Vetimong would like to go away to school. The young man agreed enthusiastically and readily promised to maintain secrecy about his proffered education, even to his parents. A week later, and by night, Prasort was spirited out of his small village and taken to Nakornpanom. There he was turned over to a small band of people who rowed him across the Mekong River into Laos. The party was met by members of the Pathet Lao.

Then began a long journey. Alternately walking and riding in jeeps, being relayed from one Pathet Lao walking team to another, Prasort made his way across Laos, through the jungles, over the mountains into North Viet Nam. The North Vietnamese then took over the journey. Some three months after he left home, Prasort found himself at the Hoa Binh Training School, some forty miles outside Hanoi. Approximately one hundred other Thai students were also there.

For a year Prasort Vetimong was given rigorous courses in elementary reading, writing, mathematics, Communism, and guerrilla warfare.

"I was taught," Prasort said to me, "that Americans hate one another; that they kill all the people who are not white. I was also told that the Americans had taken over my country, that this takeover was part of the imperialist's plot to occupy Southeast Asia. I was also taught," he continued, "that the government in Bangkok was run by tyrants, that I must come back home and help give my people economic and political freedom. My orders were to come back to my village and contact members of the Communist Party central committee in my district. That was the first time I knew there was such a thing."

Prasort Vetimong is far from stupid; much of what he told me must be weighed against the fact that he had been captured by government forces, that he was under a possible death sentence when he talked to me. I am certain he knew very well what the struggle was about as he made the long three-month trip back to his village.

"Once I returned home I explained my absence by saying I had just been going around." ("Going around," simply wandering around Thailand, living off the land and the people, is a kind of coming-of-age among teen-age boys of the back villages. It is something of a wild fling, and every Thai village boy lives for the day when he will be old enough to do it.)

"Then," Prasort continued, "I followed my instructions and contacted the central committee of the Communist Party. I was assigned to get more recruits."

He set about recruiting his fellow villagers for insurgency activity, but his activities came to light when a local girl alerted the police. Prasort was promptly arrested; he told all, even the names of the members of the central committee in his area.

"Did your parents come and visit you in jail?" I asked.

"Yes," he replied.

"What did your father say when he found out?"

"My father was also arrested."

"Why?"

"Because he was a Communist."

"Did you know that your father was a Communist?"

"No."

"Did he know that you were a Communist?"

"No. We kept secret from each other. These were our orders. Only the committee knew who were Communists."

Prasort is, of course, purging himself, trying to escape punishment. It will be said that he doctored his story in an attempt to save his life. I was deeply concerned about his credibility. For example, Prasort said the Communists at the Hoa Binh Training School had told him that the Americans were using the Thai bases to bomb Viet Nam.

"Do you believe it?" I asked.

"No," he shouted back. "It was all a lie. I know the Americans are not using my country to bomb anybody."

The Thai security officer who had brought Prasort, under guard, for the interview with me went into a rage. "My God! Doesn't he know that what they told him is true?"

I began to doubt what Prasort was telling me. Then I asked him to define Communism.

"Communism," he replied, "is a government under which all men are equal; there is no black or white, no rich or poor. Everybody votes and decides what shall be done. That is the kind of government we should have in Thailand."

The Thai security officer looked embarrassed. Nobody has voted in Thailand for twenty years. Doubt as one will, there can be no question that Prasort Vetimong had been lifted from peasant ignorance into alert political awareness in less than a year. There is something else that must not be forgotten: Prasort Vetimong had been scheduled to join Phathisawata in the mountain jungles of northeast Thailand.

Runners provide a continual communication between Rassamee and Yod. Their classic method is simply to come down from the mountains to a small town and commandeer a taxi, forcing the driver, at gunpoint, to take them where they wish to go. If the driver makes trouble, they kill him; if not, they take his cab and leave him stranded on a backwoods road, miles from home. Working in concert, then, Rassamee, Phathisawata, and other insurgency leaders have created the current crisis in the northeast. Here is a summary of the government report on insurgency activity for the last week in December 1966:

Insurgents surrounded four villages in the easternmost provinces. They forced the villagers to endure long speeches denouncing the government, then they demanded rice. Under the cover of darkness, the insurgents vanished into the jungles.

In yet another province, the combined Thai army-police unit arrested seven members of a "shadow play" group which was traveling from village to village acting out Communist propaganda in the guise of the popular form of open-air entertainment.

Elsewhere, the insurgents raided a village and extorted three hundred dollars from the poverty-stricken inhabitants. (The average annual income in the villages is thirty-three dollars.)

They also burned out a bridge over a small creek in Nakornpanom province, thus making it difficult, if not impossible, for back villagers to get their vegetables to market. Police and insurgents clashed twice, six days apart. One terrorist was killed; a carbine, eleven bullets, and one hand grenade were captured.

Police overran two insurgency hideouts near Udorn; thirty Communist documents were seized along with three hundred pounds of food, and packages of clothing. In both instances the Communists retreated, leaving trails of blood.

American and Thai officials report that the assassinations of village officials by the Communists in the northeast alone occurred at the rate of ten a month during 1966. There were thirteen hundred such killings in Viet Nam in 1961, the year the United States became deeply involved there. But the biggest Communist conquest in Thailand to date cannot be documented in a report; rather, it is written in the hearts of the villagers—fear, naked and justified fear.

By late afternoon of the day I visited the police station in Na Kae, I was in Tatparnom, an exquisite northeastern town some fifty miles away. My taxi had developed carburetor trouble. Several Thai mechanics were laboring to correct the problem when an excited bus driver sped into town and announced that the Communists had just struck in Ban Papark, fifteen miles away, and killed the chief of police.

Sing Korn, my interpreter, and I spent the next half-hour trying to find a taxi driver who would take us to Ban Papark. They were all terror-stricken. Finally one driver agreed to take us to Ban Papark for three hundred bahts—fifteen dollars—a month's income for him.

The road to Ban Papark was dusty, bumpy, winding, and narrow. Yet the driver moved along at sixty miles an hour. I felt ostracized because Sing Korn and the driver kept chattering in Thai. I knew the driver was desperate about something but I could not get Sing Korn to make immediate translations. Finally he explained:

"The poor man is scared to death; he only agreed to drive us because his wife and son are sick; they need medical care and he cannot afford it. But this trip will pay for the bills."

Suddenly the driver slammed on his brakes; the car literally skidded a full circle along the the middle of the bumpy, dusty, back-village road. I leaped from the back seat and immediately realized what had happened. A bridge some thirty yards ahead of us had been destroyed by the Communists. We backed up, drove onto a side path that ran along the bottom of the creek, and emerged onto the road some fifty yards beyond the burned-out bridge.

Ban Papark had closed its doors and gone to bed even though the sun was not yet down. Upon our arrival the police surrounded our car. As soon as we told them of our mission, they explained that the incident had indeed happened, but in Koodta Kai, ten miles farther on. But the Communists had burned the bridges along the village roads. There was no way for me, or the police, to get to Koodta Kai. There was no alternative but to go into Nakornpanom, the district center.

At twilight we reached Nakornpanom, and it was only when we saw an American soldier, a Negro from Mississippi, patrolling the road, that we felt safe.

In Nakornpanom itself, all of the official representatives from Bangkok were gathering at the Temple to arrange for the burning of the remains of the chief of police who had been assassinated at Ban Papark.

THE ENEMY WITHIN

His name is Cheon Rachivons, and he stood there, in my room at the Grand Hotel in Nakornpanom, speaking into the tape recorder. As the police lieutenant in charge of investigating subversion, Cheon knows more about the magnitude and nature of the Communist insurgency than any man in his province. I had sought him out the night before. He does not have a telephone; no one in Nakornpanom, the most sophisticated city in the northeast, has a phone. But every driver knows exactly where the lieutenant lives. My Thai interpreter and I rented a pedicab, the modern equivalent of a rickshaw,* and made our way down the pitch-dark street that led to Cheon's home.

"I cannot talk to you tonight," Cheon said with regret. "I must go to your hotel and meet with your CIA and CID men. I can come to your room in the morning."

As we rode together back toward my hotel, I discovered that Cheon's rendezvous with the American intelligence people was to take place in the room three doors down the hall from me. Indeed, I remembered the three Americans well; we had shared lunch tables in the hotel café that day. I was as curious about them as they were about me; we asked each other questions. Nobody got honest answers. After all, they certainly would not confide their CIA status to me, and I was not anxious that strangers know I was searching out Communist insurgents.

"I will see you in the morning," Cheon promised as we drove up to the hotel. "*Shawardi*—good night."

It was still early in the evening and Nakornpanom was yet alive. The marketplaces bustled with sellers and buyers, the stores and tailor shops were doing a brisk business. Curious Thai peasants from the back villages ogled at expensive radio and television sets priced at many times their yearly income. The cafés and streets were jammed with American servicemen; heavy American Air Force trucks lumbered through the narrow streets, all but forcing American jeeps and Thai tricycles to the curb. Thai prostitutes in the Civilized Club, known among servicemen as "VD Gulch" were doing a good business.

The moon rose, a pale pink as I walked along the riverfront a block from my hotel. The Mekong flowed quietly toward the Gulf of Siam; across the river one could see the lights in the small villages of Laos. It was difficult to believe that I was standing in a hotbed of Communist

---

* The driver sits on the front seat and pumps the vehicle. The passengers sit on a large back seat capable of holding three people. The vehicle is commonly called a "pedicab."

insurrection. Yet the facts were inescapable. Three-fifths of Laos is under the control of the Laotian Communist Party, despite the shaky neutralist government established there in 1962. Military flare-ups between the Communists and the rightists are a frequent occurrence in Laos, and the Thais of Nakornpanom gather on the riverfront to watch the deadly fireworks. Then, there is that section of the Ho Chi Minh Trail that winds through Laos, providing the North Vietnamese with access to South Viet Nam. Despite cries that we are violating Laotian neutrality, America has been bombing the trail for over two years.

The political turmoil of this section of Southeast Asia is in such stark contrast to the land's natural beauty that I felt as I did when I visited Kenya seven years ago: here is the land of God, He made a masterpiece of it; then He made man, and man made a mess.

Overhead there was the almost constant chopping din of American helicopters. Some of them were ferrying Thai soldiers into the jungles; others were headed into North Viet Nam to rescue American flyers downed there. Frequently there was the whining roar of American jets.

Then, "boom!" The earth shook, the tables in the waterfront café rattled, almost upsetting my dinner.

"What the hell was that!" I demanded. The Thais who had joined me for dinner were embarrassed; they nervously fingered their sticky rice and remained silent.

"Boom!" Again the earth shook and the tables rattled.

"If you really want to know what that is," one of my Thai dinner companions said acidly, "ask the American flyboy you had dinner with last night. He is doing it."

My Thai interpreter motioned me to silence. Then he leaned toward me and quietly explained:

American bombers were returning to their bases in Thailand after a day of raids over North Viet Nam; ofttimes the Americans were unable to drop all of their bombs, and rather than run the risk of landing with the dangerous explosives still aboard, they were jettisoning them into the jungle belly of Laos. The people of Nakornpanom always know when the American jets are returning; they see a small American plane take off and then circle high over Laos. The plane is piloted by the flyboy I had had dinner with; his job is to guide the returning jets to the spot where they are to unload their bombs.

"Is the area inhabited?" I asked Sing Korn, my interpreter.

"No," he snapped. "The people have been moved out. But it is hell on the animals!"

"Boom!" The earth shook, the tables rattled.

The overflights, of course, are a clear violation of the Geneva Agreement that ended the Laotian war in 1962—a remarkable negotiation carried on by John F. Kennedy through Averell Harriman. The jettisoning of bombs into Laos is an even more egregious violation of the Geneva accords. But all parties concerned—the Laotians, the Thais, and the Americans—have agreed to pretend it just isn't occurring.

Not that America is alone in defying the treaty. Hanoi has some thirty-five thousand men stationed along the Ho Chi Minh Trail in troubled Laos. These North Vietnamese have forced the Lao who once occupied the farmland near the trail to flee to the American-controlled sector of Laos. Now the Vietnamese plant the rice fields, they feed and guide the Vietnamese soldiers as they make their way down from North to South Viet Nam.

Southeast Asia is a land where nobody plays by the rules, where nobody makes promises he intends to keep. It is a land of shaking ground and rattling tables.

Promptly at seven the following morning Cheon Rachivons knocked at my door.

"I must speak quickly," he said, unfolding his prepared statement. "I must hurry to take a helicopter flight into the jungles. We have just now, a few minutes ago, received word of Communist activity." I started the tape recorder and handed Cheon the microphone. He read his statement in the dialect of the northeast:

"The summary of Communist activity in Nakornpanom area: Nakornpanom is an important major city of northeast Thailand. Right on the border between Thailand and Laos, with over two hundred kilometers of common border between the two countries, Nakornpanom consists of eight *amphurs* [districts] and three hundred thousand people. The majority of the people are farmers and rice growers. The main crop of the region is tobacco.

"The people of this area share a common heritage, similar customs and language, with their Laotian neighbors. There has been steady and free exchange of trade, customs, and travel between the two peoples since time immemorial. The common trait of the people is their kindheartedness and a warm welcome extended to all visitors, foreign and otherwise. Everyone is welcome in the true, warm Thai hospitality.

"But now this honor toward others is beginning to undergo gradual change. This is due to the appearance of a group of people who are joining a foreign power and inducing young able-bodied men and women of this town to travel to North Viet Nam and China for indoctrination in Communist tactics and insurgency. This includes training in the use of weaponry. Then these Communist-indoctrinated people return to cause trouble and sabotage.

"In 1961, about five months before the coup of Kong Le in Laos, there was an operation conducted here by a Lieutenant Kong Sin [alias Nai Kam], who operated an insurgency force on both sides of the Mekong River, between Laos and this town. He belongs to the Laotian Communist forces [the Pathet Lao]. They set up their headquarters in Thailand at Bang Nong He and Bankoot. This Nai [Mister] Kam set up business as a doctor, without the benefit of a license to practice. He used his doctor's office as a front; his real job was to recruit Thai men in the villages and send them to Hanoi and China for Communist training. He recruited many men, but we caught him. He is now in jail in Bangkok and his case is before the Thai courts.

"Soon after Nai Kam was captured, one Nai Yod Phathisawata appeared on the scene. Nai Yod is now the leader of the Communist cell. This Nai Yod is a man from the city of Chacheont Sao, near Bangkok. He attended a good school in Bangkok called Suan Khlab. He has been living in the Na Kae area district for about twenty years. He also lived in the Communist part of Laos, Viet Nam, and China. He once managed a sawmill, but now his business is in the jungles of the mountains where he directs the insurgents.

"The Communists are all around us," he concluded. "We are afraid and concerned."

Question: How long do you think it will take to end the insurgency?

Answer: At least five years, if then.

Question: How many men does Nai Yod have?

Answer: We are certain he has at least one hundred hard-core followers with him in the jungles. We don't know how many silent supporters he has in the villages. They farm by day and shoot by night.

Question: How many men do you have?

Answer: That is classified information; it cannot be divulged.

The interview was over. Cheon Rachivons stood impatiently in the middle of the room. "Give him two hundred bahts [ten dollars]," my Thai interpreter whispered to me. I paid gladly; not only was the information valuable but I was well aware of Cheon's plight: he risks his life daily, he is poorly paid. There are months when he is not paid at all.

A typical Thai, Cheon spoke in polite understatement. The plain fact is that Thailand and Laos are on the verge of a major confrontation.

Northeast Thailand fronts on that section of Laos that is under the tight control of the Communists, the Pathet Lao. The majority of the peoples in the northeast are Lao; but, to repeat, they are Thais and their loyalty to Thailand is beyond question. However, the physical similarities between the Thai Lao and the Laotian are such that it is impossible to tell them apart. Thai Laos frequently cross the Mekong into Laos in search of work and find no need whatsoever to identify themselves as Thai. In return, Laotians cross into Thailand to work and market their fish. There is no reason for them to identify themselves as Laotian.

Thus it is that ethnic similarities and easy access have provided the Communist apparatus with an ideal line of communication between Communist Laos and northeast Thailand. Lieutenant Kong Sin, the unlicensed doctor of whom Cheon spoke, is a classic example. Kong Sin is Laotian; he worked in concert with Kong Le, the general who started the coup that plunged America into war in Laos. That same Kong Sin is now the Minister of Defense in the Laotian government.

Counterinsurgency activity by men like Cheon, then, becomes an endless exercise in trying to determine just who is loyal and who is not. There is no doubt that Laotian infiltrators are deeply involved in the insurgency in the northeast; they provide communication lines, supplies, leadership, and money. But they are only part, and a minor part at that, of the problem. The most dangerous fifth column inside Thailand are the North Vietnamese.

To understand this, one must recall history, go back to the days when Ho Chi Minh was leading the Vietnamese people in their struggle against the Japanese during the Second World War, and then against the French during the colonial uprising that led to the present American-involved war. Ho's struggles against the Japanese and the French were unbelievably bloody and barbaric affairs; entire villages were destroyed, the people killed. As Ho and his men moved down from the north, the Japanese and the French were moving up from the south. Hundreds of thousands of Vietnamese, largely in the north, were caught in the closing circle of fire and death. They fled, over the Ho Chi Minh Trail, into Laos and then—most of them—into Thailand.

It must be remembered that the government in Bangkok was in dire straits at the time. Thailand had accepted a Japanese presence of sorts, and had actually declared war on the United States. Bangkok officialdom had little, if any, time to spend dealing with the flow of North Vietnamese refugees into northeast Thailand. Meanwhile, the North Vietnamese came across the Mekong River in droves, some forty thousand of them.

The refugees took up squatter's rights on land they carved from the edge of the jungles between Nakornpanom and Na Kae. They set up village life, with their own police and their own government; they perpetuated the language and customs of North Viet Nam. A remarkably frugal people, they deliberately ate less than they should, eschewed entertainment, and saved their money. They never became Thai citizens.

"All the Vietnamese did," a Thai official remarked to me, "was to till their fields and stay home and have babies."

The refugees succeeded remarkably at both enterprises. They now rival the Chinese as businessmen in the northeast; their population has almost doubled. Shortly after World War Two the Vietnamese refugees were given a stout leg up when the International Red Cross flooded them with money, food, and clothing—while the equally poor Thais continued to live on the edge of starvation. Politicians from the northeast demanded that Bangkok clear the refugees from the territory. The matter wound up in the United Nations and an attempt was made at repatriating the refugees. The attempt failed because the North Vietnamese feigned ignorance of their background. To a man, they all swore they had no idea where they came from in Viet Nam; they insisted further that they did not wish to be caught in the hostilities between the French and Ho Chi Minh, and later Ho Chi Minh and the Americans.

Like most issues affecting the northeast, the government in Bangkok simply chose to ignore the matter. Bangkok did order the refugees to close their schools, disband their police, and become a part of the Thai nation; but these orders, of course, have not been obeyed. The schools merely went underground and the young ones continue to be taught that they are Vietnamese, to speak Vietnamese and Chinese; the police still come out at night and protect the Vietnamese villages; and the refugees have made few steps toward integrating themselves into the Thai way of life. It is simple to spot their establishments—the Krong Throng Hotel and the Leng Hong Restaurant in Sakolnakorn; the exotic camera shop just across the street from the Civilized Club in Nakornpanom. One can also easily spot their villages. The homes are built flat on the ground; the Thais build on stilts. And, as I have already pointed out, the North Vietnamese eat dogs; the Thais don't.

Now, twenty years after they first came to Thailand, the refugees are deeply rooted in the life of the northeast. Whereas the original refugees never became Thai citizens, their children, the so-called "born people," are Thais. There has been some intermingling and a good deal of intermarriage between Thais and Vietnamese. But, the Vietnamese are still fiercely loyal to Ho Chi Minh.

The Thai government did not realize the full danger of this bomb in its belly until the Communist insurgency burst into full bloom some five years ago. Then the evidence began to mount: captured Thai insurgents confessed that they received some of their orders by radio, from the commercials on jazz programs sponsored by businessmen in the northeast. There is no longer any commercial radio in Thailand. And it is now common knowledge that Vietnamese are ferrying young Thai dissidents across the Mekong into Laos where they begin the long journey to the Communist training schools in Hanoi and Peking.

"We know who these North Vietnamese are," a top Thai official who asked that his name be withheld, said to me. "We can tell them from their looks. But we cannot always recognize their children. We have warned them. They cannot organize or have group meetings. If things get much worse, we will have to put them in compounds as you Americans did to the Japanese. They are not really welcome here any longer."

Thai Premier Thanom Kittikachorn openly made the same point in June of 1967. "We have definitely decided to evacuate the North Vietnamese," he said, "and we have been in negotiations with the South Vietnamese government on this subject. We don't yet know if the Saigon government will accept them." But on the same day Premier Thanom made his views known, the Saigon embassy in Bangkok announced that the South Vietnam government would not allow the refugees in its territory because the refugees are committed to, and under the control of, Hanoi.

The entire refugee question has now evolved into a very curious and dangerous situation. The town of Udorn offers a clear example: there are upward of four thousand North Vietnamese refugees in this town of fifty thousand people. The refugees remain as unobtrusive as possible, yet Hanoi still maintains a Red Cross office in the center of the town's business district. The refugees canceled their annual celebration of Ho Chi Minh's birthday in 1967, and many of them are employed at the huge American airbase less than a mile from Udorn—a base from which American aircraft daily bomb the outskirts of Hanoi.

The refugees have no intentions of going home to Hanoi. Indeed, Nguyen Van Tuong, the North Vietnamese who has directed the Udorn Red Cross center since 1964, flew to Bangkok to lodge a formal protest over the Thai government's decision to evacuate the North Vietnamese. The results of his talks with high Thai officials are not known, but the prevailing opinion in Bangkok is that the Thai government has little alternative but to allow the refugees to remain. Much of the problem is of the Thai government's own making since they refused to let the refugees become citizens.

"Most of the refugees, particularly the young ones, would like to settle down and become citizens," an American official said. "It is probably too late now."

A Thai provincial official seemed bemused by it all as he remarked, "If we only had an island big enough to hold all of the refugees . . . but we don't." Then he shrugged his shoulders, smiled, and walked away. The North Vietnamese refugees, like the Thai peasants, are perched on their enclaves in the northeast. They are festering, ripe for Communist exploitation.

"The Communists are only taking advantage of a situation that has existed for years," Tuam Na Nakorn, the mayor of Nakornpanom, said to me. "I am fifty-eight years old and have lived this issue all my life. The government in Bangkok has treated the people of my area like dirt; how dare they now wonder why the people are not loyal to Bangkok. Why should they be?

"I can remember the days when every politician who fell out of favor in Bangkok would be banished up here to be our district officer; we have the worst schools, the lowest income, and we get the bottom of the bucket when money for roads is appropriated." Tuam Na Nakorn (his name means he is the son of a former governor of the province) paused while he took a long, deliberate sip of whiskey. "I was once head of the labor union here. The government abolished that because we were trying to get better wages and working conditions for the people. Everything we tried to do to help the people was ruled out by those bastards in Bangkok.

"Go ahead and write it down," he told me. "I am one man in the northeast who is neither a Communist nor a puppet for Bangkok. I am now the head of my town. I know what is going on. They are spending thousands of bahts building fancy buildings for Bangkok's district offices up here; but nothing is being done for the people. At least a thousand men from my town are now either up in the mountains with the Communists or working with the Pathet Lao over across the river."

Then, "boom!" The earth shook and the chairs on the mayor's front porch rattled.

"You Americans have accomplished something no foreigners have been able to accomplish in the history of Thailand," the mayor lectured me. "We have always been a free people—that is what the word 'Thai' means; we escaped colonialism; we outwitted the Japanese. But now America has taken over our country. I am very sad about it all."

Tricycling back to my hotel, jogging along the main street past the Vietnamese-owned shops, I recalled something I had read preparatory to my visit to Thailand. During a July 1966 seminar on Thailand, William J. Gedney, an expert on Thailand and Professor of Linguistics at the University of Michigan, wrote:

"If I were a northeasterner, and saw the great numbers of Thai and American tanks and armored vehicles and heavily armed men cruising up and down my streets and highways, at a time when the Bangkok government seems to have difficulty providing ordinary police protection against highway robbery and banditry, I believe I would wonder to what extent this military power was there to protect me from the Vietcong and the Pathet Lao, and to what extent it was there to keep me in line.

"Finally, if I were a northeasterner, I am not sure how much interest I would take in all the programs and discussions on the northeast that one hears so much about these days, since they emanate from Bangkok and Washington. I might regard it as ironic that it is only now, when governments in these two places are concerned about their political interests that my area has aroused so much concern."

My day ended early. I had hoped to see the governor of the province and the district officer. Neither has a telephone; and when I went to their respective homes I discovered that they were in the Buddhist Temple, at the cremation service for the policeman who had been killed in Koodta Kai a few days before. I returned to my hotel to find a crew-cut press officer from the nearby American airbase waiting for me. He had come in response to my request for permission to visit the base and talk with servicemen.

The press officer was a pleasant but nervous fellow; a Texan and just out of journalism school, he looked at me over the top of his beer and explained that both the American and Thai governments were determined to keep reporters off the base. "We let an NBC television crew on one of our bases," he explained. "We didn't like what they did with the film when they got back home. Now, nobody but service personnel can come on base."

THE SECOND FRONT

Late in January of 1967, Thai counter-insurgency troops raided a Communist camp deep in the jungles of Thailand, only twenty miles from the city of Betong.

Even the Thai troops were shocked by what they discovered: the camp contained thatched huts for two hundred people; there was a more than ample supply of weaponry and other implements, indicating that the Communist campers had settled down to a village life of farming and insurgency. The camp was littered with Communist propaganda leaflets along with excerpts from the writings of Mao Tse-tung and handwritten manuals on guerrilla warfare. There were only two "white people" in the camp; they were stuffed-dummy likenesses of Uncle Sam and John Bull, toys which the Communists used for playing darts in their spare time. Throwing darts at Uncle Sam is a readily believable pastime for the Communist insurgents in the northeast, but such hostility toward Great Britain is unheard of along the banks of the Mekong. Alas, the raided camp was not in northeast Thailand; rather, it was some one thousand miles from Nakornpanom, in the extreme southern end of Thailand, just across the border from Malaysia. With this discovery it became irrefutably clear that the Communist insurgents now have strong footholds along both the northeastern and southern tips of Thailand. Even the government in Bangkok, located in the precise middle of the country, admits they now have trouble on two fronts.

South Thailand, geographically, is a sunswept strip of Siam that lies below the Isthmus of Kra, that fifty-mile-wide neck of village-dotted land that separates the Gulf of Siam from the Andaman Sea. One-fourth of all the Thai peoples live there, and—with the exception of rice farming, of course—they eke out a living from the rubber growing and mining. In the hierarchy of neglect by the central government, the northeast comes first, the south second. And one has to take but a single look at the peoples in such southern villages as Betong, Sadao, and Marathiwat to realize that history has dealt Thailand a serious ethnic and religious blow, that the insurgency problem in the south is potentially far more dangerous than that in the northeast.

Eighty-five per cent of the peoples of the four southern provinces are Thai-Malay, with deep cultural roots in Malaysia. They are Muslims to the marrow of their bones and they speak Malay. The second largest ethnic group are the so-called "Bangkok Thai," who are Buddhists. The remainder of the population is Chinese. The Bangkok Thai are the government officials, the governors and civil service officers; the Chinese are the merchants and middle men, holders of the economic power. There are a few Chinese peasants. But most of the peasants are Thai-Malay, the most deprived of the poor. All of the government officials are appointed by Bangkok, and in a country where there is no vote, there is little for the Thai-Malay to do but endure oppression at the hands of a tiny minority. As with the northeast, political posts in the south have traditionally been reserved for neophytes or those politicians out of favor in Bangkok. Only recently, for example, has the solidly Thai-Malay Yala District been assigned a governor who speaks Malay. This self-serving arrangement worked well for Bangkok since the turn of the century—until thirteen years ago, when trouble started.

During the war, the British colony of Malaya (now Malaysia) was overrun by the Japanese. The guerrilla warfare against the Japanese was carried on mainly by Malay-Chinese under the leadership of a taut Mao strategist called Chin Peng. Chin and his top associates were trained in Peking and they received the bulk of their supplies from the China mainland. Chin allied himself with guerrilla forces inside Thailand, just across the border, who were carrying on a struggle against the Japanese. These Thai and Malay-Chinese guerrillas fought brilliantly, contributing much of the Allied victory in Indo-China. But while the world was praising Chin Peng's military prowess, it forgot to examine his politics.

At the cessation of hostilities the British covered Chin with decorations, including the Victoria Cross. The naïve British hope was that Malaya would resume its colonial status, that Chin and his force would become members of the British colonial regulars. Instead, Chin turned his guns on the British and undertook the conquest of Malaya. Taking to the jungles and employing the tactics that had worked so well against the Japanese, it seemed, for a while at least, that Chin was about to deliver England a stinging and embarrassing defeat.

The British reacted with a massive show of power, however. They threw forty thousand men into the conflict, seasoned troops aided by jungle-trained Gurkha warriors, Australians, and New Zealanders. At the height of the conflict, Chin had some five thousand men fighting with him in the jungles of Malaya. His supply line to China effectively cut, Chin's forces were decimated by superior British power, hunger, and disease. Seriously ill and badly beaten, Chin gathered the remnants of his once proud forces—an estimated five hundred men—and crossed the border into Thailand where he joined with the Thai Communists and set up operations in the jungles along the border between Betong and Yala.

That was twelve years ago, and whatever dreams Chin had of returning and conquering Malaya vanished with the formation of the Federation of Malaysia in 1963. Instead, Chin reorganized his forces and set upon the destruction of the goverment in Bangkok by capitalizing on the unrest among the Thai-Malay and the Chinese.

Chin's appeal to the Thai-Malay was a promise that when the government in Bangkok was destroyed, they would become a part of Malaysia. This promise of separatism from Thailand struck a deep and responsive chord with the oppressed Thai-Malay, whose land—in the days of the Sultans and before the British conquest—was more Malaysian than Thai.

Chin's appeal to the Chinese in the south is ethnic as well as economic. Whereas Bangkok Chinese have merged into Thai life, even to the point of intermarrying and taking on Thai names, the Chinese in the south have remained a group apart. The relationship between the Chinese in the south and Bangkok is one of the most critical ethnic problems in Southeast Asia. Economically, the Chinese feel—and rightly so—that they are being taxed without having representation.

Chin has not been seen since late 1966, and there is wide speculation that he is dead, that the movement has been taken over by dissident Thais who were trained in Peking. Regardless of the leadership, it is indisputable that upwards of a thousand hard-core Communist insurgents are lodged deep in the rugged hills along the Thai-Malay border. They are tenacious; they tend mountain gardens, vanish when pursued, and frequently shoot members of the Thai-Malay border patrol from ambush. Like their cohorts in the northeast, the insurgents in the south prey upon the farmers and merchants in the back villages, some of whom are Chinese. Thai government spokesmen now admit that some twenty-five thousand villagers willingly support the insurgents.

In their early years—under Chin—the insurgents appealed mostly to the Thai-Malay and the Chinese. Recently, however, Thai government agents have collected pamphlets and other materials discarded by the insurgents which show the Communists are making an all-out appeal to Bangkok Thais. Their literature attacks both the Thai and the American governments, blaming them for the economic drought that has hit the southern tip of Thailand. The crisis has been caused by the depressed price of raw rubber, the principal product of the area. The Communists charge that the "American capitalists" are responsible for the fact that the price of raw rubber is now one-fifth that of the Korean War peak. But it is the issue of racism, pyramiding anti-Chinese attitudes and activities, that provides the Communists with their best argument in southern Thailand. And the Thai government itself has actually handed the Chinese the sharp weapon of racism. It must be remembered that the insurgents, both Malay and Thai, are mostly Chinese. The Thai government seems to believe in guilt by association, because it assumes that all Chinese are disloyal. This has led to the vicious abuse of loyal Chinese in southern provinces, such as Yala.

Jack Foise, the Thailand correspondent for the Los Angeles *Times,* wrote this revealing passage from southern Thailand:

"Because the Chinese here work hard and are both thrifty and smart they are resented. The Chinese sense insecurity and make desperate gestures of acquiescence, such as foregoing chopsticks for the Thai-favored knife and fork. The Chinese uncomplainingly make payoffs to Thai officials as a price for doing business and making their personal lives serene."

Thus it is that the Chinese, the Thai-Muslims, and a growing segment of the Bangkok Thais are bitterly anti-Bangkok. Chin's disappearance has greatly increased the insurgents' following; for an outsider—Chin is Chinese-Malay—could never really gather serious support among the proud and boastful Thais. But now that indigenous Thais are being secreted into Red China and then back home to assume leadership, the insurgency is becoming "home-grown" and gathering support. Southeast Asia experts estimate that the situation in the south approximates that in Viet Nam ten years ago.

"The insurgency in the south is gathering momentum," a State Department official said to me. "We must stop it now or it will lead to real trouble. We don't want another Viet Nam-type involvement."

The Chinese are Thailand's most important minority group—socially, economically, and politically. They began pouring into Thailand early in this century and they now number some three million. One Thai out of every ten is Chinese, the exact numerical ratio between Negroes and whites in the United States. Southeast Asia, as I have commented, is scarred by anti-Chinese racism, but Thailand has earned the reputation of being the most liberal state in that area. Now the crisis in the south is about to upset the delicately balanced relationship between the Bangkok Thais and the Chinese Thais.

The Chinese came to Thailand upon invitation, as construction workers for the building of canals and railways. However, the Chinese brought with them their commercial brilliance and soon took advantage of the then exploding world rice market. The Thai rice farmers sell their rice to a Chinese who, in turn, sells it to the government; the government puts the rice on the world market. Much of the Thai government's annual income is earned in this manner. While the Thai peasantry concentrated on farming and the Thai middle class preoccupied itself with scrambling for white-collar government jobs, the Chinese took over the basic economy of the nation.

The early Chinese immigrants assimilated quickly; they married Thai women and took on Thai names. About 1910, however, Chinese women began to flow into Thailand. They set the stage for the tightly-knit Chinese community now threatening to erupt. The Chinese rapidly set up their own schools and social welfare organizations. By 1914 the Thai elite had become alarmed at their growth and influence and declared a "Chinese problem." Since 1932 the control of Chinese economics and politics has been an implicit policy of all Thai governments. Today, all Chinese schools as well as social organizations are banned. Chinese must now attend Thai schools and speak Thai. Their societies are banned under the same rule that outlaws all political groups.

Until recently the "Chinese problem" was more a matter of the group's size and economic strength than of politics. Of the three million Chinese in Thailand today, only seven hundred thousand were born in China. The majority were born in Thailand; they are Thai, they speak Thai, but have managed to maintain their Chinese culture despite the efforts of the Thai government. Although the Chinese have never used their formidable economic power cohesively—and certainly not for political ends—they have never escaped the watchful eye of the government in Bangkok. There was grave concern during World War Two about the Chinese, but they proved able to accept the fact of Thai-Japanese collaboration. The establishment of Nationalist China on the island of Taiwan provided another anxious moment; the Thai government delayed its recognition of Taiwan several years for just this reason. But the apprehensions were ill-founded. The Thai Chinese made no overtures to Chiang Kai-shek. The rise of Red China, however, set the stage for the current crisis. After all, so many dissident Thais were—and are—being spirited to Peking for training that the Bangkok government began to seriously distrust some members of the Thai Chinese community.

But until now the Thai Chinese have never been seriously threatened. Although the Chinese secret societies and social service organizations are banned, the Thai government has chosen to ignore the groups' underground operations. Young Thai Chinese are forbidden to learn Chinese in school, yet the Thai government is aware that most young Chinese speak and write Chinese fluently. I stood in a bank in Nakornpanom and watched as the Chinese manager calculated the conversion of my traveler's checks into bahts in Chinese, and then translated the information into Thai, for the teller.

The situation in the south today is a new development;

this kind of flagrant anti-Chinese attitude has deeply shaken the entire Chinese community in Thailand. It is inconceivable to Asian experts that wealthy Chinese in Bangkok, Nakornpanom, Sakolnakorn, and Udorn will continue to smile and bow while their fellow Chinese in the south are subjected to an increasing degree of abuse. Thus, the spark now flying from the anvil of racism in the south could well ignite all Thailand. Concerned over growing Chinese unrest, the Thai government rescinded its twenty-year-old ban on Chinese-language instruction in May 1967. But this has done little to assuage the Chinese who are being brutalized in South Thailand. The move certainly did not appease the insurgents; late in June the insurgents boldly announced the creation of a "third front" in central Thailand, some two hundred miles from Bangkok.

BANGKOK, THE CITY-STATE

The pincers are closing on Bangkok, the city-state, the seat of Thailand's central government, and the font from which all economic and political powers flow. The city itself is the pearl of Southeast Asia—perhaps, as many people feel, the only thing in that section of Asia really worth fighting about. As one walks along its bustling streets, stares up at its many-storied buildings, and gawks through the windows of its well-stocked stores, it seems almost mythical that fifteen hundred years ago the entire city of Bangkok was beneath the waters of the Gulf of Thailand. The waters receded, and today Bangkok is a glittering jewel perched on the Chao Phy River, twenty-five miles upriver from the gulf, and the place some two million people call home. Bangkok is also the home of the Southeast Asia Treaty Organization, the United Nations Economic Commission for Asia and the Far East, and the regional headquarters for several other United Nations agencies as well. The city of Bangkok is reassuring; a billboard reads "Bank of America Welcomes you to Bangkok." It works: I walked into the Bangkok Bank of America and borrowed five hundred dollars on my Bankamericard. Another billboard reads "You have a Friend at Chase Manhattan." That works also: a friend of mine entered that bank and within five minutes cashed a personal check on his New York bank. The entire façade is one of prosperity and stability. Even as one paddles along the city's canals, where feces bob up and down like cork at a fishing festival, it is difficult to feel deep concern for the poor who live along the banks and in houseboats, for they are all gathered in their small living rooms watching television. The police are polite, the taxi drivers are embarrassingly courteous, and one is much safer along the streets of Bangkok at night than he would be in New York, Chicago, or Los Angeles. Yet something is wrong, menacingly so. Everybody knows it, but nobody talks publicly about it. To find the seat of the wrong, one has only to traverse the full length of Bangkok's main street, Rajadamnern Avenue. At one end of the avenue is the Royal Palace; at the other end, the House of Parliament. Along the way one will find a myriad of government buildings.

To the eternal embarrassment of the American government, which has committed men, money, and political fortune in the land of Siam, Thailand is a mean, military dictatorship, dedicated to the proposition that the function of the government is to let the people enjoy life so long as they don't express a desire to participate in the process of government. The people have no legal rights whatsoever; newspapers are censored and public gatherings for political purposes are outlawed. Agitation for free speech and political activity can—and will—get one jailed, or even shot.

"Your country must have lost all sense of moral commitment," a well-educated Thai said to me privately, "to use Thailand as a base to send bombers aloft in order to bring freedom to Viet Nam. If America is really committed to bringing freedom to Southeast Asia, you should start by bombing Bangkok!"

Bangkok intellectuals as well as Thai peasants hear of elections in Laos and even in Saigon; their proud spirits wilt. "The Lao and Vietnamese were once under colonialism," the Thai intellectual noted. "We have always been a nation, a free people; we are politically more sophisticated than they are. If they can vote, why can't we?"

The honest answer to his question lies with Field Marshal Prapas Charusathira, Thailand's strongman, who said: "To hold elections too soon would be like wrenching a child untimely from the womb. The thing to avoid is undue haste." And when Senator J. William Fulbright denounced the military dictatorship in Thailand from the Senate floor, Prapas observed to a foreign diplomat that it was shocking that Fulbright was so concerned about individual freedom in Thailand when the Arkansan cares so little for the rights of black people in his home state.

In Thailand, whenever one speaks of the government, he means Bangkok. All officials, even in the remote, neglected provinces, are appointed by the military triumvirate that runs the country from Bangkok. The Communist insurgents are moving into the breach, which has its roots in two centuries of history and customs.

The history of modern Thailand could well be told by

beginning with the overthrow of the absolute monarchy in June 1932. But this must be briefly stayed until some background of the spiritual and psychological relationship between the masses and those in power is given.

Premodern Thailand, the Thailand of Anna and the King of Siam, centered around the king who lived in his splendorous palace in the center of Bangkok. The masses worshipped the king; even his ministers prostrated themselves before him. He was a man of mystery, of great supernatural powers; he seldom ventured from the palace. When he did, it was a regal pageant by land or on water, and the king was surrounded by soldiers and police. Such was the power and majesty of the king that King Chulalongkorn, who reigned until 1910, was given this title:

> Most excellent royal foot which is a glorious decoration for our hair; king wearing the great crown of the angel; royal descendant of the sun who shines like the finest jewel, most excellent of lineage, monarch as supreme as the greatest emperor of the worlds; greatest sovereign of righteousness, supreme king of men, King Chom Klao the second, lord of Siam including the north, the south, and all the lands nearby which are Lao, Malaya, Karen, and many others.

To an American all this is ridiculous. To the Thai, however, it makes complete sense. For the politics of Thailand are rooted in the concept of the God-King, a concept common to both the Hindu and Buddhist traditions. According to this view the entire universe is a single moral order of related elements. The center of the universe is the holy mountain, Meru, surrounded by oceans and continents, one of which is the dwelling place of men. Meru itself is the dwelling place of the gods and they are ranked in ordered levels of power and virtue. From this flows the concept of the state, or the kingdom, which must be an exact replica of the great universe. Thus, the Royal Palace becomes the holy mountain (Meru) and the king is a surrogate god. The king's wives and ministers, the palace, the city, and the state are organized according to astrological systems so that they will have a proper relationship to the great universe. More, and this is the heart of the matter, once the masses accepted this notion of the state, they also embraced the belief that the people of high rank were militarily more powerful and morally better than ordinary men.

Preoccupied with rice farming, the Thai masses became even more devoted to the God-King concept when their rulers successfully led them through a blood war with Burma and then kept them from falling under the colonial conquests of the French and the British, or both. It was greed, not God, that saved Thailand from colonialism. During the last decade of the 1800s, the French moved into Viet Nam and Laos and paused on the Lao side of the Mekong River. Meanwhile, the British were moving up from Malaya. Each was determined to protect its colonies from the other. Through a complicated diplomatic maneuver, in which the government of Bangkok performed brilliantly, it was agreed that Thailand would remain neutral, independent, and a buffer zone between the two aggressive Western powers.

Thailand entered its modern moment with the people harboring a deep spiritual conviction that high rank is to be equated with power and virtue. Indeed, many of the kings spent years as Buddhist monks to lay a valid claim to a virtuous life and good works. But a group of Thai intellectuals educated in Paris rejected the God-King idea. That was the beginning of today's difficulty.

The drama of 1932 centered around four men, dissident Thais who from time to time have joined together, only to split apart and then reunite once again. The principal personality in the drama is Pridi Phanomyong, the man who actually sparked the 1932 coup and now directs the Communist insurgency from exile in Red China.

Nai Pridi Phanomyong, the man who is now bent upon the violent overthrow of the Bangkok government, was born in Ayutha city of a Thai father and a Chinese mother. The elder Phanomyong, a middle-class landowner and farmer, was widely read and something of a scholar. With backing from his father, Pridi scored brilliantly as a student in the secondary schools at Bangkok and won a scholarship to study in Paris at the famed Ecole de Sciences Politiques. It was in Paris that Pridi first saw free men participating in the process of government. In the Paris of the twenties and the thirties, dissidents from all over the world—American writers, Latin American refugees, Africans irate over colonialism, disgruntled Asians—gathered in small, dark bars to bemoan the state of affairs in their homelands. The Thai students were no exception. Pridi and his friends gathered after classes to brood about the God-King in Bangkok. One night they translated their brooding into action and formed the People's Party, a clandestine political group committed to work for the reform of government in Thailand. It is still not known just how many Thais participated in the formation of the Party, nor is it known who they were. But one of the principals—Luang Pibul Songram, a close friend of Pridi's—was destined to play a role almost equal to Pridi's in future developments. The Thai students were certain that their education in France would assure them high government posts once they returned home—an integral part of their plot. From these positions they planned to bring about the overthrow of the God-King. That is exactly what happened.

Pridi returned to Bangkok in the early twenties and joined the Ministry of Justice during the reign of Rama VI. The time could not have been more propitious for what Pridi and his Paris conferees had in mind. Thailand was inching toward modernity and its simplistic internal economic and foreign policy was proving unequal to the strain. Much of the problem lay with the personality of Rama VI himself. The first Thai monarch to be educated abroad, Rama VI ushered his kingdom into a colorful period during which the upper class of Bangkok was introduced to such alien ideas as Western dress and cotillions. Rama VI was also, in effect, the founder of intellectual nationalism among the educated class. A prolific writer of essays on national devotion, he attacked the Thai Chinese for their growing separatism. (This was the beginning of the "Chinese problem" in Thailand.) Rama VI took his absolute position seriously and ran the Thai government as a one-man operation. This angered his royal relatives and top ministers who had also been educated abroad and who thought that their views should be given consideration before matters of internal policy and foreign relations were finalized. Rama VI died in 1925 without a male heir; he did bequeath the nation, however, to a small band of top government officials who were bitterly at odds with the Royal Palace.

Rama VII, the king's youngest brother, came to the throne because he was next in line. Whereas Rama VI had been a flamboyant and strong monarch, Rama VII, who never expected to be king and had not prepared himself for the task, was reserved to the point of shyness. The royal princes and ministers who had become disgruntled under Rama VI assumed control of the policy making of the government.

Pridi, meanwhile, had functioned magnificently as leader of a group of Paris-educated lawyers in the Ministry of Justice who were assigned the task of giving Thailand its first codified laws. So outstanding was Pridi's work that Rama VII bestowed upon him the title of Pradith Manutham—writer of good laws. But Pridi was doing more than writing laws. Working underground, Pridi and his Paris friend, Luang Pibul Songram, who had risen rapidly in the army and was then a major in Thailand's artillery corps, effectively organized the People's Party and patiently waited for the proper moment to strike.

The moment came as a result of the kind of Palace-Bangkok intrigue that has plagued Thailand for centuries. At some risk of oversimplification, this is what happened. Two dissident groups combined to bring about the coup—the older army officers provided the military force and the younger military officers and civil officials provided the ideology and the zeal. The older army officers were led by Colonel Phraya Phanon, a Prussian-trained militarist who was deeply angered because his advice on military matters was not heeded by the prince who headed the Thai military. The younger group was led by Pridi and his Paris conspirator, Pibul; the third leader of the younger group was Khuang Aphaiwong, also one of the Paris founders of the People's Party.

Early in June of 1932, Rama VII left Bangkok for the seaside resort of Hua Hin. At dawn on June 24, even before the markets were awake, the commanding general of the first military district of Bangkok, along with the "King's Guard," rolled out their tanks and surrounded the Royal Palace and all major government buildings. Leaders of the coup then seized all key positions in the city of Bangkok and arrested various high government officials. The king was forced to capitulate and he accepted the invitation to rule under a constitution. The People's Party surfaced, declared itself the provisional government, and set out to form a government acceptable to both the king and the Party. Praya Mano Prakorn Nititada, a well-respected judge who had not participated in the coup but was sympathetic to its objectives, was named Prime Minister. Leaders of the coup were given top cabinet posts. Pridi became head of the Legal Committee of the Revolution. His task was to write Thailand's first constitution.

The constitution, which Pridi had been secretly drafting for years, was quickly completed. Rama VII proclaimed the document law on December 10, 1932, less than six months after the coup. The document was strikingly similar to the constitution of the Third French Republic, which had impressed Pridi so deeply. The king was stripped of all power to take independent action; there was to be a single legislature, with the royal Cabinet responsible to it. The constitution also provided that there should be a period of tutelage before full democracy would be introduced to Thailand. For ten years, or until half of the eligible voters completed four years of school (whichever came first), half of the parliament was to be appointed by the People's Party. The other half was to be elected by adult suffrage. Thailand seemed well on its way to democracy. But it was not to be. And it was Pridi who executed the first of a series of political moves that were to wreck the new government and the People's Party as well.

The People's Party executed the coup of 1932 under a six-point manifesto:

1. Freedom of the people in politics, law, courts, and business.
2. Internal peace and order.
3. Economic well-being and work for all by means of economic planning.
4. Equality of privileges.
5. Freedom and liberty not conflicting with the foregoing.
6. Education for all.

Pridi, then Minister of Justice, interpreted the third item of the manifesto—economic well-being and work for all by means of economic planning—as a mandate to issue his Economic Plan of 1933 for all of Thailand. The People's Party government was less than six months old when Pridi walked onto the floor of parliament and read his white paper—an economic plan for the nation. A shocked parliament, composed completely of middle-class Thais, listened as Pridi outlined an economic plan that would have nationalized all natural and industrial resources, including land itself. The people, with a few exceptions, would all become employees of the government.

Shouts of "Communist!" and "Bolshevism!" rang through the house. The resentment toward Pridi reached such proportions that Praya Mano Prakorn, the compromise Prime Minister, elected to close down Parliament and rule by decree. A sweeping law banning the Communist Party was enacted and Pridi was banished to a small post in the Paris embassy where he sulked in obscurity for two years. Then began a series of plots, counter plots, coups, and intrigues among top government officials.

Mano Prakorn, the Prime Minister who forced Pridi out of the country, was actually a front man for Pibul, who became commander of Bangkok's army and finally replaced Prakorn as Prime Minister.

Pibul promptly recalled his old friend Pridi from Paris and installed him as Minister of Justice. Pibul became an absolute dictator and set out to steer Thailand clear of the war that was raging in Europe. He gained great public aclaim when he forced the tottering Vichy government to restore Laos, which Thailand had lost during the delicate negotiations that kept Thailand from falling under colonialism. But on December 7, 1941, Pibul's luck expired. The Japanese landed along the coast of southern Thailand and demanded that Pibul either permit passage of Japanese troops enroute to Burma and Malaya or fight.

"Which side do you think will win this war?" Pibul asked his Cabinet during a tense meeting. "That is the side we are on."

The Japanese were given free passage through Thailand; Pibul actually went through the motions of declaring war on the United States and accepted the Japanese stationed in Thailand as "friendly allies."

Pridi, meanwhile, had been concentrating on the Thai intellectuals and the rapidly expanding civil service corps. He founded Thamasat University, which became the training ground for both Rassamee and her father. Pridi also gathered the support of the Thai navy, which was constantly being overshadowed by the army and air force. During the period of Japanese presence, Pridi, in addition to making life difficult for the Japanese, gathered a hard-core, well-equipped underground force with the full support of the neglected Thai navy.

The armistice had hardly been signed when—in what is now known as the army-navy game—Pridi struck with force, toppled Pibul, and put his fellow Paris conspirator in jail for war crimes.

But Pibul was imprisoned under an ex post facto law and lawyer Pridi knew it. He released Pibul and exiled him to France. The quarrel between the two men blew over, and in less than a year, Pibul returned from Europe as a senior statesman and was given the title of field marshal.

Pridi held absolute power, without even the indirect interference of the king. Rama VII had gone into exile during the furor that followed the announcement of Pridi's Economic Plan. He was succeeded by sixteen-year-old Prince Anan Mahidon, who, in turn, fled to Europe for schooling during the war years. Pridi took advantage of his power to give Thailand a new constitution. As free people, the Thais participated in a general election and sent members to speak for them in a bicameral legislature. Political parties functioned openly; three of them gained national stature, and it took the combined efforts of two of them to keep Pridi in power.

Then fate once again turned on Pridi. His government was beset by corruption, the ill that afflicts all Asian countries. But the real blow came on the morning of June 9, 1946, when young King Rama VIII, who had just come home from Europe, was found dead in bed, a .45 cal. U.S. Army bullet between his eyes. Some said suicide, others charged murder. But a charge of regicide was more than Pridi's government could withstand.

A trial of sorts, with all evidence given behind closed doors, was ordered. Only a few close-mouthed men know what was said and heard there. Some say that the king's younger brother, Prince Bhumipol, who was sleeping in the same room with the king, was responsible for the murder. Indeed, the prince was shipped off to Switzerland. However, the king's private secretary and two high chamberlains were shot for regicide. Lieutenant Sithichai was also implicated in the king's murder, but he fled to Red China before he could be tried.

A crisis of confidence gripped Thailand. The king was too powerful a symbol for his death to remain unexplained. Public confidence in Pridi was badly shaken and he attempted to correct the situation by asking Pibul to assume military control, hopefully to serve as a stabilizing force in an hour of national crisis. Instead, Pibul used his power to force Pridi out of office. But that was not the end of the matter.

Several days later, Pibul, in full pomp and circumstance, appeared for the dedication of the American dredge *Manhattan.* The entire diplomatic corps, including the American ambassador, turned out for the ceremony. Naval officers loyal to Pridi surrounded Pibul and forced him aboard the navy flagship, *Ayudhaya.* While his navy supporters were carrying out the abduction before the shocked array of diplomats, Pridi himself was commanding a dissident army faction as it stormed the Royal Palace. The Thai air force, however, moved in to support Pibul and began to bomb the Thai navy into submission. Indeed, Pibul escaped from the *Ayudhaya* only minutes before the vessel was bombed to the bottom of the sea. The Manhattan Affair, as the Thais call it, was over. Pridi had lost. With the aid of close friends, Pridi obtained a navy patrol boat and sailed for Red China.

That was late in June of 1951. Pridi Phanomyong, the man who had kept Thai politics in turmoil for more than two decades, was gone but he is still the patron saint of educated Thai. Shortly after arriving in China, Pridi set up the Thai government-in-exile which directs the Communist insurgency in Thailand today. Even with Pridi out of the country, the Bangkok government was to know little political peace.*

Early on the morning of November 30, 1951, General Sarit Thanarat, commander of the Bangkok army, and General Phao Sriyabon, director general of the police, joined with Prime Minister Pibul in announcing over the radio that the Thai constitution was revoked. The Thai peoples, politically, were now where they were in 1932.

In 1955, Prime Minister Pibul visited the United States and told us how good things were in Thailand. But Pibul was in deep trouble at home. Caught between two powerful and ambitious military men—Sarit and Phao—Pibul decided to allow some of his people to exercise the freedom he had seen in America. He decreed free speech, allowed the newspapers to engage in partisan politics, and even turned Bangkok's central park into a "Hyde Park" where all politicians could express their views. Political parties, with the exception of the Communists, functioned openly.

Pibul won the election of February 1957, but charges of corruption made certain the results would not be allowed to stand. On September 16, Sarit rolled out his tanks. Parliament was dissolved; the constitution was suspended; Pibul fled the country; Phao went into exile; and Sarit's deputy, General Thanom Kittikachorn, became Prime Minister, largely because Sarit was ill. He soon

* Those interested in a more detailed account of Thailand's modern history should read *Politics In Thailand* by David Wilson.

left the country for the United States where he received extended medical treatment.

Once again a healthy man, Sarit returned home in October 1958, resumed command of the army, and carried out a bloodless coup in which he established himself as military dictator of Thailand.

Sarit lived happily and reigned absolutely until his nonviolent death in 1963. He is best remembered for his flamboyant ways and for his total corruption. He did nothing to restore constitutional government in Thailand.

General Thanom Kittikachorn resumed the prime ministership in December 1963, and promptly filed suit against one of Sarit's concubines for the return of state money, jewels, and property. Thanom, as of this writing, is still Prime Minister.

But the real power in Thailand today is "His Excellency Deputy Prime Minister Prapas Charusathira, Minister of Interior, Commander in Chief of the Royal Thai Army and Deputy Supreme Commander of the Royal Armed Forces." Prapas is also "Chief of the National Police Force" and of the "Village Defense Corps," which protects the peoples in the northeast and the south from the Communist insurgents.

As for the people of Thailand—and I am deliberately being repetitive—*there is no constitution; no one can vote; martial law prevails; it is a felony punishable by death for more than five people to gather and talk politics.*

Bangkok, the city-state, is a strange place where strange things are commonplace. At night the windowshades are tightly drawn and radio sets are tuned to Radio Peking. Thousands of Thais listen intently as the voice of an old man says: "This is the voice of free Thailand. People of Thailand rise up; throw out the dogs who rule from Bangkok; force the filthy American imperialists from our homeland."

The voice is that of Pridi Phanomyong.

WAITING FOR THE MESSIAH

The worshipers sat transfixed as Buddhist monk Lunk Phaw Yi entered the pulpit of Dong Takawn Temple in the small northeastern town of Pachip. It was mid-June of 1966; word had spread throughout the area that an astounding miracle was to be performed that Sabbath day. Lunk Phaw Yi ("Uncle Father Two"), moving as if in a trance, extended his empty begging bowl toward the uplifted faces of the worshipers. Then he covered the bowl with a small cloth and began to pray. Moments later Phaw removed the cloth, and the crowd gasped: the bowl was brimming over with rice. The worshipers, stirred to exaltation, broke into muffled shouts of "Pee Boon! Pee Boon!"

The following afternoon, Phaw went into the village and placed a fishnet against a tree. That night the villagers slept in expectation. Their anticipation was rewarded; the following morning, the net contained a gold fish. "Pee Boon! Pee Boon!" the people shouted as the village of Pachip assumed a festive spirit. Officials and police representing the government in Bangkok knew they were in for serious trouble. They decided to discredit Lunk Phaw Yi as quickly as possible. The gold fish was sent to a goldsmith in Bangkok for analysis. But the result was hardly calculated to restore calm to Pachip: the fish was solid gold.

Bangkok became alarmed. They dispatched a special officer, a man trained in the strange religious ways of the northeast, to witness and evaluate Phaw's miracles. Phaw entered the pulpit the following Sabbath, and fully aware of the policeman's presence, proceeded to cause another empty bowl to overflow with rice. The rice was topped by a gold leaf.

"Take this to the director of the division of religion in Bangkok," Phaw said as he handed the bowl, along with the rice and gold leaf, to the startled policeman. The leaf also proved to be gold and the policeman became a supporter of Lunk Phaw Yi. The matter culminated with Phaw being brought to Bangkok for a glowing ceremony under the sponsorship of the Bank of Bangkok.

This report was confirmed by Tich Thieh-An, a Buddhist monk who was living in the home of the policeman when the incident occurred. Tich Thieh-An is now special adviser to the Thailand Project at the University of California at Los Angeles.

Most Westerners view such doings with suspicion, but few Thais would. For the miracles of Lunk Phaw Yi fulfill the deep promise of the strain of Buddhism that pervades all Thailand. And the Thai police, indeed, had just cause for concern. Ten years ago a similar series of miracles were performed by a monk at Mae Phong. There were shouts of "Pee Boon," and by the time Bangkok took note, the monk had gathered several hundred followers who took up arms and set off a religous insurrection against the Bangkok government. Had the insurrectionists been as well-steeped in military tactics as they were in religious fervor, they would have imperiled all of northern Thailand. Fervor fell before steel. The insurrectionists were slaughtered. In all, five hundred people lay dead. This revolt was the latest of a number of such uprisings that have plagued Thailand for more than a century.

Phaw is now back among the villagers of Pachip, but the Thai government is keeping a close and concerned eye on his activities.

The coming of Pee Boon, the deep religious tradition that one day a Messiah will appear and deliver the Thai peoples from evil, is a central ploy in the scheme of the Communist insurgents. To understand its danger, we must recall the history of the tradition.

The overwhelming majority of the Thais are Buddhists of the Hinayana sect. They are under the Theravat teachings and insist that they follow the lessons of Lord Buddha to the letter. They are in stark contrast to the more flamboyant and larger Mahayana sect that flourishes from Tibet to China, from Japan to Viet Nam. The key factor about the Hinayana sect is that it is Thai, that the Thai peoples have imprinted their own folkways and mores upon the general Buddhist theme.

The central tenet in Thai Buddhism is the deep conviction that the "next Lord Buddha" will soon appear. The Thai peasants refer to this as the coming of Pra Sri Arya (the "Great Glorious Lord of Civilization"), which the peoples in the south pronounce Pra Sea Arn. The peoples in the northeast have translated the same mystique into the coming of Pee Boon, which means "Spirit of Benevolence."

The ideal of every Buddhist is to live the good life of service and sacrifice. Every man has two life cycles, the good and the bad. Good deeds add to one's good cycle, sins to the bad cycle. The art is to make one's good cycle so large that the individual will be a "higher," more moral, more learned man, filled with more wisdom in the next life. This is how one becomes a candidate for the next Lord Buddha, the objective of every devout male Buddhist. If the evil cycle is greater, however, one descends to a lower level in the next life.

One also participates in the life cycles of all mankind. Should the evil life cycle of all mankind become overwhelmingly and irreparably evil, a great "cleansing fire" will come to pass. The bad will burn and the good will take over the country. This cleansing fire is a far cry from the Armageddon of Christian theology. Rather, the legend calls for a holocaust of fire and war on *this earth,* in this time.

According to the legend, Pee Boon will appear during the holocaust. He will arrive amid great musical fanfare, surrounded by a heavenly host, and will appear with the blessings of a heavenly-scented shower that will quench the fires and heal all wounds. This done, Pee Boon will set up a government among men.

And these are the signs that will attest to his Messiahship: he will be able to fly; he will work miracles; he will cause stones to float. He will be a man of great military accomplishments. Indeed, he will have vanquished the foe (the bad people) and set the good people free.

Pee Boon in earthly government is a combination of the American Constitution and the promise of heaven as set forth in the New Testament. All men and women will be absolutely equal in every way. No longer will there be rich and poor; all man's material needs will be satisfied from the magic wishing trees located at all four corners of the compass. "All you do," a devout Buddhist explained to me, "is go to the magic trees and state your wish. It will be granted."

The majority of the Pee Boon uprisings have occurred in the impoverished and neglected north and northeast. The pattern is always the same. A monk works a miracle and then goes on to lay claim to the Messiahship. The simple peasants work themselves into a fervor and launch a series of atrocities and plunders that one member of the Thai royal family equates with the Mau Mau. Once the followers of the Pee Boon claimant have sufficiently terrorized the back villagers, they attempt to take over the larger villages and towns. It is at this point—at least is has been until now—that the zealots clash with the Bangkok-controlled police and go down to defeat. The so-called Pee Boons have been executed—most on the gallows, several before a firing squad.

"If I were out to overthrow the Bangkok government," a brilliant Thai intellectual said to me, "I would come as Pee Boon." When I pressed him as to just how he would accomplish the miracles required for his acceptance, he took me seriously.

"All right," he began, "let's do it. In this day of transistor radios and miniature tape recorders, I would have no trouble landing with a din of heavenly music surrounding me. As for flying, I would get myself one of those individual jet kits your military men use to fly a hundred or so yards at a time. My accompanying heavenly host would be men supplied by Rassamee or Yod. There is no difficulty working miracles for the back villagers in this day of dried and frozen foods. The Communist insurgents have already set the stage psychologically for my military victories. By killing the village officers and policemen, the Communists now control at least a dozen Thai villages—psychologically. They are convinced that the Communists are invincible. I would simply extend and enlarge that psychological terror. . . ."

But as the Buddhist troubles in Viet Nam well prove, it is all but fatal to examine the religious fervor of Southeast Asia in Western terms. After all, Yod Phathisawata served as a monk during his five-year sojourn in Laos. It is difficult to determine to what extent the insurgents are employing the Pee Boon legend. This is partly because the Thais are reluctant to discuss the Pee Boon legend freely with strangers; in addition, both Thai and American officials fear that open discussion of the subject may set off a Communist witch hunt in the Thai Buddhist movement. Such a public debate could—and probably would—plunge Thailand into a deeper civil crisis than the Communists themselves have been able to create. The Thai government has elected to treat the Pee Boon claimants as imposters, evil men who would fulfill a holy promise through sinful deeds. This tactic works well in Bangkok where some Thai sophisticates tend to scoff at the legend. But the back villages in the north and the northeast are another matter.

I first heard of the Pee Boon legend while I was in the jungles of northeast Thailand. My inquiries were greeted with a sort of sacred silence. Even Bangkok officials suggested that I could spend my time more profitably than chasing down legends. Some idea of the mystery and strangeness that surrounds Pee Boon can be gained from the following incident. Shortly after I returned to the United States, I approached professors on the Thailand Project at the University of California at Los Angeles and asked them about the legend. These men have spent years in Thailand on special grants from the United States government; two of them functioned as civil servants for the Bangkok government. Not one of them had heard of the Pee Boon legend. One of the professors, Michael Moerman, decided to raise the question with Tich Thieh-An, a Buddhist monk now in residence at the University of California at Los Angeles. Thieh-An not only confirmed the legend, but cited several examples of how it had been used to engender insurrection or separatist movements.

Another Thai intellectual visiting the United States willingly gave me an assessment of the danger inherent in the Pee Boon phenomenon:

"There is no question that the Communists are playing upon the legend," he said. "There has been clear evidence for five years that the insurgents have been telling the people of the back villages—among other things—that Pee Boon was coming soon. You must remember that these people have been expecting the Messiah for more than a century.

"The Pee Boon legend is similar to all other such theological promises. People who live in squalor and deprivation are anxious to believe that some divine superperson is coming to deliver them. It is their way of rationalizing their powerlessness, their inability to do something about their plight.

"The people of Thailand, particularly in the northeast," he continued, "have more of a psychological basis for such expectations than most people of the world today. The Communists only have to point to the neglect by Bangkok, the corruption of district officials and police, the manner in which the police have extorted staples and other goods from the peasants to show that mankind's evil cycle is now beyond redemption. Then you must remember that the back-village peasants see and hear the American aircraft as they roar overhead. Few of them know what this is all about. First of all, they don't know anything about Viet Nam; secondly, the Thai government has steadfastly refused to inform the Thai people of the fact that American bombers are stationed in Thailand. Thus all this activity in the air brings on a great feeling of mystery. And it is but a short jump from mystery to miracles.

"The Communists present themselves to the peasants of the northeast as forerunners of the deliverance that is to come. They promise that with the overthrow of the government in Bangkok, and the ouster of the Americans, that indeed everybody will be equal. There will be no rich or poor, everybody will be happy, and it will no longer be necessary to wade in the water up to one's knees ten hours a day to reap a living from the bottom of a filthy rice stream.

"Yes," he said, "the big push will come under the leadership of some kind of Pee Boon. The Communists are not stupid enough to think that they can rally Thai peasants in the name of Karl Marx or Mao Tse-tung. The real spark will come from a Thai, from a man whose Buddhist credentials are unimpeachable. He will be a man of the earth and the rice fields; he will speak the dialect of the people."

My Thai friend smiled. "All peoples have a Pee Boon," he added. "You Americans had one in 1776. You called him —and still do—the Father of your country. Ho Chi Minh is the Pee Boon of Viet Nam; this is why you will never win there. Kenya has a Pee Boon. He led the Mau Mau and now is Prime Minister of the country. Nkrumah of Ghana called himself 'savior'—Pee Boon. He led his nation to freedom. The most recent Pee Boon to appear in the Americas was Fidel Castro. When he made his triumphant march into Havana, the people shouted and worshiped, as did the followers of Jesus on Palm Sunday. In Haiti it is François Duvalier—Papa Doc; he rules because of voodoo legends strikingly similar to that of Pee Boon."

Those who are apt to be scornful, to dismiss all this as the naïve wishfulness of a backward people, would do well to recall two Pee Boon moments in our own history. The first is that of the Jews. In the Twelfth Chapter of Exodus, Moses is Pee Boon; the Egyptian Pharaoh similar to the Bangkok government. This Pee Boon succeeded. Not only were his people delivered, but from this legend came Jesus, the noblest Pee Boon in Western history.

One night I sat in a jam-packed, emotion-racked Harlem meeting hall and witnessed a disturbing scene. The late Malcolm X, Black Muslim minister extraordinaire, was speaking.

"When I say the white man is a devil," Minister Malcolm shouted, "I speak with the authority of history."

"That's right," the people shouted back.

"The record of history shows that the white men, as a people, have never done good."

"Say on, Brother, say on."

"He stole our fathers and mothers from their culture of silk and satins and brought them to this land in the belly of a ship—am I right or wrong?"

"You are right; God knows you are right."

"He brought us here in chains—right?"

"Right."

"He has kept us in chains ever since we have been here."

"Preach on, Brother Minister, preach on."

"Now this blue-eyed devil's time has about run out."

The people leaped to their feet, rejoicing.

"Now the fiery hell he has heaped upon others is about to come down on the white man."

"All praise due to Allah!" the people shouted.

"God—we call him Allah—is going to get this white, filthy, hog-loving beast off our backs," Malcolm promised.

"Say on—yes! yes! yes! . . .

"God is going to hitch him to the plow and make him do his own dirty work."

"Yes, yes, say on!"

"God is going to take over the garment district and make those white dogs push their own trucks."

Men in the audience jumped up and down and shouted their approval: "All praises due to Allah. Praise his holy name!"

"Now, now," Malcom said, "calm down, because I want you to hear me. Now I want to tell you who God is. I want you to understand who Allah is so you will know who is going to get this white, dope-peddling beast off your back."

Malcolm smiled. A ripple of laughter ran through the audience. "You see, you know who Allah is; you know who God is; you know just who is going to get the white man off your backs. The Honorable Elijah Muhammad teaches us that God—Allah—is not a spook; we don't worship any ghost for a God. We don't believe in any dead God."

"That's right."

"Our God is a live God."

"Yes."

"He is walking around here with you, among you, in you."

"Yes," the people shouted back.

"God is black, like you; God is oppressed, like you; he looks like you; he acts like you; he walks like you; he talks like you . . ."

By this time the people were back on their feet, cheering. But Malcolm had gone as far toward describing God as he would go for a while.

"Now," he said, "you have to listen with understanding to know what I am talking about."

"We with you."

"We don't let white devils in our meetings."

"No, no, no!"

"But we have to worry about some of you, because the white man has messed up your mind so bad that some of you will run back and tell everything. That's why we can't tell you everything; that's why you have to listen carefully and with understanding if you are going to find out just who God is. But if he walks like you, and looks like you, and talks like you, and suffers like you; and if he is with you, in you, and all around you . . . then . . . well, you figure it out!"

The people, particularly the men, lifted their voices in a long shout, for they had been told that the black man, taken collectively, is God—Allah—that Allah will soon, now, destroy the devil, the white man.

Malcolm X, as he did three or four times each week, had made it plain. He told black men that they—as God—must deliver themselves from the evils and hurts of the white man. And that, of course, is what they came to the temple to hear.

Malcolm is dead, the Black Muslim movement is waning. But—and here is the point to ponder—if the American Negro were ever driven to the point of desperation and the majority accepted this concept of the black Pee Boon, then on the day of the cleansing fire, every white family with a Negro cook would be poisoned.

My Thai friend was correct. Every oppressed people have their Pee Boon. They suffer and wait for the miraculous day when they will have the leadership and the manpower and the arms needed to take them to the Promised Land—where all are equal and toil is supplanted by a wave of the Lord's hand.

Prior Pee Boon uprisings in Thailand have failed, as I have already noted, because they were long on religious fervor, but short on arms and military training. Their central weakness was that the leaders were men who really believed they were the Messiah, that bullets—as the legend also promises—could not harm them. Now all this has changed.

Rassamee knows very well who she is. Yod Phathisawata knows very well who he is. Their followers know well who they are, what they are doing, and why. Yet, they too have a Messianic complex; they believe Buddha has sent them to deliver Thailand from Bangkok and Washington. They are armed from the magic trees that bloom in China and Russia. There is no heavenly music they cannot order from Radio Peking, no mission to fly which cannot be accomplished by a helicopter sent in from Laos. Their military victories are already established. One day, stones—iron boats—will float, and empty rice bowls will be miraculously filled with bags of rice from China.

And [cries of] "Pee Boon!" all mingled with gunfire, will resound throughout the land.

THE COMMITMENT

Jack Foise, the brilliant Los Angeles *Times* correspondent in Bangkok, has a strange relationship with his brother-in-law. They are both democrats and liberals of a sort, but they never talk foreign policy.

"I don't ask my brother-in-law about foreign policy," Foise told me, "and he doesn't talk to me about what I write. That way we keep peace in the family."

This is indeed a good arrangement. And in September 1966 when Foise broke the story that the United States was ferrying Thai troops into the jungles to fight the insurgents, the State Department underwent a collective, if mild, heart attack. Secrecy was part of the price we offered the Thai government for use of their airbases. Our diplomatic ties with Thailand were severely strained during the days just after the Foise article. Pressure mounted from a myriad of sources as both governments issued half-hearted denials.

"But I have to give my brother-in-law credit," Foise said, referring to Secretary of State Dean Rusk. "He never called or cabled me. When we did talk, he asked me about the weather in Bangkok."

Dean Rusk may not attempt to influence what Jack Foise writes, but the American embassy in Thailand does. Shortly after I arrived in Bangkok, an American diplomat asked me about Foise's reliability. I explained that I had never met Foise, that I only knew of his work.

"Did you know that Foise was kicked out of Viet Nam because he broke story deadlines?" the official asked. When I said I had no knowledge of the incident, the American diplomat warned me to stay clear of Foise during my visit in Thailand. Instead of avoiding Foise, I decided to research the incident. This is what I found:

Foise covered an American operation in central Viet Nam. With the permission of the local commander, he filed his story. The United States Information office charged Foise with misconduct, arguing that he filed his story without clearing with the Saigon office. When Foise replied that he had the permission of the local commander, the Saigon office countered by saying it was not sufficient. Foise's press credentials were lifted for thirty days, with the approval of General William Westmoreland.

This seemed harsh treatment indeed. But the punishment appears less unusual when one recalls that only a few weeks before, Foise had written a story proving that a Viet Cong atrocity story issued by the Information Service was an out-and-out lie. The matter was so embarrassing that no more daily reports were issued on "enemy atrocities."

Rather than endanger its contacts with American sources, the Los Angeles *Times* transferred Foise from Viet Nam to Bangkok—where he promptly broke the story of American involvement in Thailand. Clearly, the American official who approached me was assigned to discredit Foise.

The Foise incident is instructive. The Johnson Administration has committed the American people to another Viet Nam-type war in Asia without seeking the advice or consent of either the people or the Congress. Thus, American writers move to the brink of angry criticism as they attempt to inform the American public that they are in yet another war. But this is the risk run by men such as Jack Foise and Maynard Parker, an American Army officer who became the Hong Kong correspondent for *Life* magazine. Their writings were the direct cause of my opting to go to Thailand when it became clear that my invitation to visit Hanoi had been withdrawn. Moreover, the work of these men alerted the American people to the fact that their money was being spent and their sons called upon to die for a cause that was unclear.

Late in 1965, Maynard Parker and other American Army officers were called into Bangkok for a top-secret briefing. Employing a long pointer and a map, the major in charge outlined the battle plan the United States would use if the Communists attempt to invade Thailand from Laos. Then came the question period: one officer wanted to know how much barbed wire he should order to defend our bases; a major from the Quartermaster asked how much gas would be needed to fuel our tanks and trucks. Finally, Parker asked what we would do if the Communists started a war of liberation *inside* Thailand.

"We do not expect a guerrilla war in Thailand!" the major snapped.

Only the tragedy, the bloodshed and the deaths, keep this episode from being high comedy. More than a year earlier Radio Peking had announced that a war to overthrow Bangkok was underway in Thailand. In 1964, Chinese Foreign Minister Chen Yi happily told a diplomatic reception, "We now have a war of liberation going on inside Thailand." During the same year, back-village police and other officials were assassinated and government police discovered hidden caches of arms and provisions in the jungles.

One would expect that the American briefing would have been concerned with the obvious Communist insurgency. Instead, as Parker says, few Americans—civilian or military—were particularly concerned. "There is not going to be war here; the Thais are our friends," Americans in Bangkok were saying. They also repeated things like: "The Thais are happy; they have rice to eat and there are fish in the klongs."

Even more startling is that when I visited Thailand in the winter of 1966-67, Americans said much the same thing to me. "I just don't believe there is an insurgency movement in the northeast," said one American, the wife of a junior diplomat. "You reporters are starting your own war. Those killings up north are the work of bandits. There simply is no cause for a war of liberation in Thailand."

This incredible ignorance of the truth is a direct result of deliberate brainwashing carried out in both the American and Thai press. American Army officers sought a tour of duty in Thailand as an opportunity to sun themselves in the Gulf of Siam, to buy fine silks and jewelry for their wives, and to just plain relax. New recruits stationed in Korat, Thailand, were met by the commanding officer who bragged, "I only work one hour a day." At night the commander of our forces at Korat took to the bars and joined with the natives to play "dead bug." One drinker shouts "dead bug" and everybody falls to the floor, on his back, with his feet and arms wiggling in the air. The last man on the floor buys drinks for the house. It was seldom the commanding officer.

Meanwhile, the Communist terrorists were escalating their efforts. At Ban Renu, the village headman was shot after he had been seen talking to a policeman. In the Muang Nakornpanom area, another headman was ambushed after he had assisted police in tracking down a small band of insurgents. Military intelligence officers stationed in the northeast filed a series of reports to Bangkok, detailing the mounting terrors. "I wrote reports but never got queried on them," one field officer said. "The only time Bangkok called, they told us, 'Get on the team! You boys are the only ones writing pessimistic reports. Things are fine down here!' "

The diplomatic corps proceeded in much the same fashion. "Gee," one junior diplomat said to Maynard Parker, "I guess something should be done about the northeast." And, in what Parker describes as "something out of a Bob Hope Road movie," an American AID official arrived for an interview, floating up the river, along with his wife, in a rebuilt junk with a crew of black-pajamaed sailors manning the sails.

The Americans who arrived in Thailand full of zeal and a desire to do their jobs, either as soldiers or as civilian advisers, soon found themselves bogged down in lethargy —lethargy generated by the Americans in Bangkok and exceeded only by that of the Thais in Bangkok. The Americans ended up spending the major portion of their time on volleyball courts, counting the days to homegoing.

Major Dusty Rhoades, an infantryman who earned his credential during the Korean War, gave this account of his assignment in Korat:

"I never received a military, let alone an economic or political briefing on the northeast. I didn't know what areas were dangerous, what areas the Thais were working in, or what was going on. It didn't take too long, however, to discover that much of our aid was wrong. I was up in Surin on an operation when it began to rain. The Thais had forgotten to pitch the tent and began to work on it with a couple of beat-up hoes. I saw three brand-new American shovels lying outside, unused, and wondered why—until I finally realized that to use an American shovel, you have to have shoes to put between the flesh of your sole and the shovel. These troops didn't have any shoes.

"Of course, some of our aid is pure junk; we have given the Thais tanks that are so old that there are not even parts for them. The armor-battalion commander knows that if he moves the tanks, half of them will break down before he leaves the camp. So, naturally, he just lets them sit there. We've given the Thais single-barrel 40mm anti-aircraft guns which we didn't even use in World War Two. The damn things must be thirty years old.

"Their army is understrength because they don't have the extra money required for field pay. So they don't train, let alone go into the field to hunt guerrillas. The situation is serious in the northeast. With some direction and some money in the right places, we could probably roll it up. But all we do is play volleyball."

That was late in 1964, during the days when nobody in Bangkok, Thai or American, was concerned about the doings of Rassamee and Yod. Then something happened.

Shortly after two o'clock on the morning of February 7, 1965, the Viet Cong launched a sneak attack against the American airbase at Pleiku, South Viet Nam, killing seven American and Vietnamese and destroying thirteen American aircraft. In a matter of hours, American bombers took off from Thai bases to carry out the first major raid over North Viet Nam. Unknown to both the Thai and American peoples, their fate had been sealed.

The bombing of North Viet Nam became incessant, requiring more men and materials. F-4C Phantoms blasted off from the airfield at Takli; F-105 Thunderchiefs roared aloft from Korat. The airbase at Udorn came suddenly alive as F-101 reconnaissance planes flattened out over the Mekong River and headed for Laos and Viet Nam. SAC tankers for midair refueling blanketed Bangkok's International Airport. The American military census in Thailand increased from four thousand in early 1964 to eighteen thousand by the end of 1965. Today it approaches fifty thousand men.

The growing crisis in Viet Nam—not the growing insurgency in northeast Thailand—caused America to build Freedom Road. We couldn't have cared less about the Thais. Our only object was to service our airbases. But in the process of servicing our airbases, we drove deep into the heart of the insurgency area that had been plaguing the northeast for five years. As Parker said, "The men and machines that poured into Thailand were concerned not with Thailand, but with Viet Nam. To the Air Force, Thailand was a landlocked aircraft carrier. For the American High Command this meant the luxury of planning missions and strategy in relative calm. To the pilots it meant complete relaxation when not in the sky."

The Thais were willing to support our efforts, but they did not wish to be boldly identified with the struggle to win Viet Nam and Southeast Asia. The letter of the agreement was clear: there was to be no mention of the bombing flights from Thailand by either the American or the Thai governments. The cover story (after all, they had to tell the peasants something) was that the Americans were on "training flights," that our planes were simply "refueling at Thai bases."

The Bangkok government had little trouble maintaining secrecy. Thai newspapers dare not print things the government does not wish the people to read. But the American press was yet another matter. Ambassador

Graham Martin, perhaps the most powerful American in all Southeast Asia, assigned Bob Beecham, the press officer for the United States Mission in Thailand, to muzzle the American reporters. His job was not too difficult. Most of the American writers are stringers, men with business in Thailand other than just reporting. They certainly were not about to jeopardize their interests. The United Press correspondent was a Thai, a man who would not risk the wrath of his government by writing the truth about the planes that were roaring above his head. But the Associated Press stringer in Bangkok grew weary of censorship, and he filed a story giving complete details of the Thai-based raids over North Viet Nam. The account was carried by hundreds of papers in the United States, only to be sent back to the American embassy in Bangkok marked "top secret—limited distribution."

Ambassador Martin and Bob Beecham reacted by sealing off all sources of information within both the Thai and American governments. Then Beecham berated the reporter. "Don't write any more stories," Beecham barked, "because they are against the national interests of our country!" The correspondent continued to file stories and was subsequently reassigned to Indonesia.

The truth, however, was out. Junketing writers turned up in Bangkok asking embarrassing questions. They encountered precisely what I faced in 1966-1967. All I could get out of Bob Beecham was a press kit that had been passed out during President Johnson's visit to Thailand following the Manila Conference in October 1966. When I insisted upon more information, I was passed to the hands of Marshall Wright, first secretary of the American embassy.

Compared to Beecham, Wright is a totally forthright man. He lays it on the line, tells it like it is, and when a touchy question is raised he will say, "I cannot answer you; go out and find the truth for yourself; then come back and I will tell you if what you discovered is correct."

Even so, writers are touted away from the insurgency and the American activity on Thai bases. I was advised, instead, to write about the American assistance program for the impoverished Thais; to tell the American people of the magnificent road-building jobs we are carrying out in the land of Siam. When I announced that I was going into northeast Thailand, that I planned to talk with Thai peasants, and Communists as well, Marshall Wright was ordered by Ambassador Graham Martin to advise me not to do it. Then, a month after I returned home, I had a two-hour interview with William F. Bundy, Assistant Secretary of State for Asian Affairs, in Washington. Bundy began to speak of our Thai-based air activity, only to be interrupted by his press aide, Oscar Armstrong, who said, "That must go off the record; the Thai government would not like to have an American official quoted as having said this."

"Goddamit!" Bundy shouted back. "Haven't the Thai officials told their people the truth yet?"

The answer was "no." The Thais didn't know, nor, indeed, did the Americans know—officially.

There was much to know. America has tripled its armed forces in Thailand since 1964. Two-thirds of our bombing of North Viet Nam originates in Thailand; the entire operation of the American aid program, as well as the Peace Corps, has been converted to counterinsurgency activity, under the direct control of Ambassador Graham Martin. Ex-FBI agents serving as advisers to the Thai government's counterinsurgency team now swarm over Thailand. The CIA is there also, as they were in the days of the corrupt Sarit government, playing both sides of the street, making sure that America wins regardless of who loses in Bangkok.

I defied Ambassador Martin and Marshall Wright when I went into the remote northeast. I was followed by both the Thai and the American intelligence people. I'm glad.

They were there when things went "boom," when the earth shook and the tables rattled.

The pitiable truth is that we will never be able to convince the Thai peasants that our sudden concern about the insurgency is in their interest. Suddenly, after the Viet Cong attacked Pleiku airbase in South Viet Nam, orders went out to exhume all of the reports from American officers in the northeast that had been filed and forgotten. Maps on the walls of the American missions in Bangkok were flagged with needles pinpointing the insurgency areas. "You people should have been asking questions—these questions—about Viet Nam five years ago," Secretary of Defense Robert S. McNamara told a group of reporters in 1966. "It's too late now. Now you should be asking about Thailand. Five years ago our tactics in South Viet Nam weren't perfect. We didn't build up the South Vietnamese fast enough. There still may be time in Thailand."

But the reporters and writers did ask the right questions about Thailand. The Johnson Administration told us lies. I asked an air force press officer the right questions on the day when things went "boom," and the tables rattled.

"What was that?" I asked.

"I don't rightly know, sir," he replied, "I don't rightly know."

THE THREE-HOUR LUNCH

"Our commitment to Thailand is total and irrevocable," Ambassador Graham Martin said to me.

I paused for a long moment, partly out of shock, but mainly to offer the ambassador time to clarify his statement; he resumed the leisurely eating of his lunch.

"Does this mean our men will die, if necessary, to defend the current government in Bangkok?" I asked.

Martin's reply was instant and unmistakable: "Yes."

Marshall Wright, first secretary of the American embassy in Bangkok and my other luncheon companion, raised his eyebrows at me, as if to say, "I told you so."

"I know what you are thinking," the ambassador commented. "I have known of your liberal views for years. We had a mutual friend in Adlai Stevenson. But before you condemn your government for collaborating with yet another undemocratic government, let me tell you something about me, about the problems your government faces in Southeast Asia. Let me tell you what we are doing to resolve some of the human and social problems you seemed so concerned about."

Fortuitously, I was in Bangkok at a time when Ambassador Martin was both angry and hurt. He was angry with those Americans who travel the globe, criticizing their government and apologizing for its foreign policy. He was hurt because some American politicians have referred to him as the "colonial governor of Southeast Asia." There were things Ambassador Martin wanted to say that day at lunch, and he made it abundantly clear that he wanted me to report his views to the American people. He wanted me to write and speak with authority. Martin talked for three hours. My only choice was to listen, to trust that in the saying of his piece the ambassador would tell me some of the things I wanted to hear.

His voice soft, at times almost meditative, Graham Martin spoke of himself and Thailand as two parallel trails that finally met and entwined after thirty years. Martin grew up amid the poverty and racism of North Carolina during the era when Thailand was seething with revolution and tottering on Communism. Thailand made a futile attempt at constitutional government during the years Graham Martin was an aide to the Deputy Administrator of the NRA in Franklin D. Roosevelt's New Deal Administration, an experience that made him fully realize how poverty and discontent can erode both the individual and the national will. Martin entered the Foreign Service after the war with Germany and Japan, just as America discovered Thailand as a convenient base along our bombing route to China and began to pour money into the coffers of corrupt Thai politicians. And just prior to being assigned to Bangkok, Martin was Deputy United States Coordinator to the Alliance for Progress, with specific orders to bring political power and economic progress closer to the Latin American masses. To put it another way, Martin's job was to gently remove political power and economic advantage from the hands of the ruling cliques that have postured over Latin America for more than a century.

Graham Martin and Thailand have rendezvoused. Thailand has made an audacious commitment to the American cause in Viet Nam; Martin has committed America to what I feel is an audacious support of a military junta.

Ambassador Martin assured me that he had no illusions about the difficulties he faces as he attempts to bring Southeast Asia into the American orbit. He fully realizes the political and moral complexities that inevitably engulf a disciple of Americanism during such an undertaking. The ambassador's fear was that I would go away with a quick report based upon simplistic judgment, that I would react in horror without knowing the facts. According to Graham Martin, these are the major issues involved in the Southeast Asia struggle:

1. The rising tide of economic expectation among the masses.
2. The absence of serious commitment beyond the village and/or religious level.
3. The tyranny and corruption of existing governments—Saigon, Bangkok, and Vientiane in Laos.
4. Racial tensions between the Chinese and other ethnic groups
5. The sectional gulf—class conflict, actually—between the peasants and the middle class in the capital city.

6. The awesome U.S. military presence in the area.
7. The threat of Red China.

Thailand is America's central base of operations in Southeast Asia and the ambassador left no doubt that he, Graham Martin, is in complete command. Members of the "team" are the head of the CIA in Bangkok, the directors of our AID and Information service, and the commander of our military operations. With unusual candor, Martin referred to the Information and AID agents in the field as "my best diplomatic officers."

Graham Martin, a former faculty member of the American War College, controls upward of fifty thousand American military now stationed in Thailand. It is open knowledge in press and diplomatic circles that the American military commander in Thailand reports to Washington only through Ambassador Martin.* Thus Martin is a member of the council that makes political decisions that determine our military actions in both Thailand and Viet Nam. Martin carries out negotiations for the extension of our military presence in Thailand; he is the key to just how much aid Thailand receives and how it will be spent; he is directly responsible for the conversion of our AID and Information service into propaganda agencies for the government in Bangkok. All CIA activity in Thailand is under his direction. He sets the guidelines for the American personnel who assist the Thais in their struggle against the growing Communist insurgency in the northeast and the south. In this land of revolt and discontent, Graham Martin is providing the Bangkok government with the military protection it could never muster for itself.

---

* This was confirmed in July 1967 when Martin forced Washington to remove General Richard Stilwell from his post as American military commander in Thailand. Stilwell wished to remain and the Thai government requested that he remain there. Martin said "No"; Stilwell came home.

"The American program comes to this," Martin said. "We must stop Communist aggression in Southeast Asia; we must support stable and viable governments; we must meet the needs of the masses in such areas as politics, health, and economics. That is what we are here to do; that is what we are going to do." Then the ambassador made a blunt point: "We are here to stay. Regardless of what you liberals say, *we ain't going home!*"

Graham Martin is an American servant. He is deeply sorry that the Thais do not have the right to vote, that they have been under martial law for a decade, that they cannot gather to discuss politics. It pains him that the Thai rice farmer gets little benefit from the sale of his grain on the world market and that the salaries of Thai civil servants have been fixed as of 1957, despite that nation's growing national economy. The American ambassador is truly sorry about all these things, but his prime concern is not the peoples of Thailand. Graham Martin deeply believes that Thailand will get a constitution one day soon. He certainly hopes so. Martin's concern is with Thailand as a base for our military operations in Southeast Asia. The struggle against Communism is the only thing that really matters.

Casually dressed, in a short-sleeved shirt and slacks, Martin slouched in his chair as he eased it away from the luncheon table. Alternately closing and rubbing his eyes, he diplomatically presented the case for American policy. As Ambassador Martin spoke he knew full well that one of his top aides had given me the same argument a few nights before, and in less diplomatic language.

I had opened the discussion with Martin's aide by asking how we could justify our presence in Thailand if we would not accept a Chinese presence in Cuba. Graham's aide countered by saying that American internal political and moral ethics are one thing, that stopping Communist aggression is another. Therefore we must abandon our own principles and do whatever is necessary to stop Communism.

"You liberals want a democratic world, but you are not willing to do the kinds of things necessary to achieve that world," he said to me. "This is a dog-kill-dog world; we must kill those dogs before they kill us."

When I pressed him for the moral basis of American foreign policy, his reply was shocking:

"It all boils down to the fact that we are right and they are wrong. What we want for the world is good, what the Communists want for the world is bad. We have the right to have our missiles pointed at Russia because they are the bad guys; they don't have the right to have their missiles pointed at us because we are the good guys. The same goes for China: we have the right to be in Thailand because we are good; China doesn't have the right to be in Cuba because they are bad. We offer the best hope for Southeast Asia; that is why we are here. That is the way things are and that is the way things are going to be regardless of what we must do to make it that way."

"Suppose we have to kill Asians to do it?" I asked.

"Then, goddamit," he exploded, "we kill Asians!"

Ambassador Martin, of course, didn't speak with such bluntness, yet he passionately defended everything we are doing in both Thailand and Viet Nam. Then he reminded me once again that our present course is unalterable, that our commitment is irrevocable. Graham Martin wishes it all didn't have to happen, that history had given him a better diplomatic moment. But he is totally committed to the theology of Americanism. And once one agrees that America is God, that Communism is the Devil, then everything else follows—morally so, at least.

There is art in the manner in which Graham Martin employs language. He effortlessly constructs paragraphs out of medium-size words, but he somehow manages to convey major information without reducing the facts to precise words. Yet the listener clearly understands what it is that Martin wishes conveyed. The future of Viet Nam is a case in point. Graham Martin did not say this in words, yet he clearly indicated to me that he believes the Communists will probably control all of Viet Nam within ten years. There is little doubt in Martin's mind that Ho Chi Minh would win any national election during his lifetime. American foreign policy makers are reconciled to this probability. Yet we seek a political, rather than a military, solution to the Viet Nam conflict.

Pensively nursing his drink, Graham Martin dealt with the apparent contradiction inherent in our seeking a political solution knowing well that our military enemy would win any national election. When Washington speaks of a political solution their thinking is in terms of a divided Viet Nam; South Viet Nam would be neutralist, but heavily influenced by massive American aid and American military presence. The military presence is to be phased out over a period of time. North Viet Nam, of course, will remain strongly allied with the Communist-socialist block. This accomplished, the Geneva Accords of 1954 will become operative once more, and a date will be set for national elections. Should the conflict end in 1967, the projection is that national elections to unify all Viet Nam will take place in 1977. And it is at this point that Graham Martin is firm about the military implications. Not only are we determined to arrest the spread of political Communism, but America has elected Viet Nam as the battleground on which to destroy, once and for all, the notion that the guerrilla-type warfare developed by Mao is invincible. Our military is determined to demonstrate its superiority even though the final political solution is apt to be the same if we were to stop the killing and the dying as of this day. The Viet Cong are similarly committed, perhaps even more so. They take great pride

—Asian pride, at that—in their guerrilla-warfare expertise. They too know what the political end will be. Yet they will not come to the peace table, although this political solution could almost certainly be achieved without further bloodshed.

I interrupted Graham Martin to say that I had talked with leaders of the Viet Cong in Geneva, Switzerland, during the spring of 1966. When I asked them what kind of political solution they desired, they gave me a detailed blueprint—identical to the American desire as set forth by Ambassador Martin. The Viet Cong spokesmen went so far as to say they had sharp political differences with Ho Chi Minh. They wanted to be neutral, not allied with the "socialist countries," as they phrased it.

"I know that," Martin said. "We are heading toward some kind of end of the war. But I don't know when or where."

Toward the end of the lunch Graham Martin grew sad. The very air around the outdoor pavilion at his Bangkok residence seemed to become heavy. "I lost a son over there," he said, slowly casting a forlorn look toward Viet Nam, some three hundred miles away. "I don't want to see another American boy die there. Every night, every day, I examine my job and pain in the knowledge that American boys are dying there. But we must do it; that is the reality of our world. My boy died there," Martin continued, his voice trailing off into a whisper. "I don't want other fathers to go through what I endured."

Marshall Wright and I sat silent, stunned. We knew of his son's death at the hands of the Viet Cong. But this is a matter Americans in Southeast Asia discuss among themselves, not with the ambassador. Just the night before, I was with a group of Thai intellectuals who were speculating whether or not Martin's private loss had affected his judgment as a diplomat so directly concerned with the war in which his son had died. The Graham Martin I saw was not a man of bitterness; he has no desire for personal revenge. The Graham Martin I saw was a man of quiet and awesome power, a rare combination of the humanitarian, the warrior, the diplomat, and the philosopher. Such a man inevitably exudes both strengths and contradictions. A European diplomat who despises Graham Martin spoke to me of him as "the most brilliant American ambassador practicing today." Some Thai intellectuals refer to him as "boss man."

Then Graham Martin jarred Marshall Wright and me out of the mood he had fixed. Once again the ambassador began to preach about the stability of the Thai government. Following the deeply personal monologue about his son, the ambassador's arguments in support of the Thai military junta seemed in bad taste. I realized that part of Graham Martin's job was to send me home primed to tell the American people about the rise in Thailand's gross national product. I also realized that he must make us believe that our Thai ally is a worthy fellow. But Martin knows well that Thailand's economic viability is a direct result of American aid and presence. He also knows that the Thai government is stable because the people are held at gunpoint. The entire exercise seemed unworthy of the man.

As we walked away from the lunch, Ambassador Martin gave me a message to deliver to the American Liberal Establishment:

"Tell them to stop marching and protesting against the war in Viet Nam. The more they march the more they will achieve the exact opposite of what they want. Every peace demonstration strengthens the hands of the hawks and the Johnson Administration. Not only that," he continued, "if Hanoi doesn't come to the peace table, the bombs we are dropping over there now will be soft stones compared to what will be dropped."

Marshall Wright and I drove back to my parked car at

the American embassy, gripped by deep, internal tenseness. Two troubled Americans in a faraway land were estranged from each other, and visibly disturbed, by what they had heard. As we turned into the curved driveway that leads to the embassy, I recalled the message Ambassador Martin had given me at the end of the luncheon to deliver to the American liberal Establishment. I asked, "Am I correct that the ambassador told me to tell the American liberal community that it is defeating its own purpose by demonstrating against the war in Viet Nam; that we just *might* drop the big bomb if Hanoi doesn't come to terms?"

"That is exactly what he told you," Marshall Wright replied. "But will you write it? Will you say it as you go lecturing on university campuses across the country?"

I promised Marshall Wright I would spread the gospel according to Graham Martin as it had been revealed to me.

Baby, I have kept the faith!

THE COMMUNISTS SPEAK UP

The stunning Thai lady who sat across from me during dinner at Nick's Number One, Bangkok's best restaurant, was a Communist. She, along with four other Thais (three men and a woman), directs the Communist underground movement in Thailand. I never could have found her. She found me. However, I was not surprised when the phone call came, telling me to go to the restaurant at six o'clock and sit alone, that I would be joined for dinner. I had let it be known in the northeast that I wanted to hear the insurgents' side of the story. A waiter in Nakornpanom approached my table and told me to expect a call when I returned to my Bangkok hotel.

"I agreed to talk to you," she began, "after I read in the paper that you had been diverted from Hanoi, that you were taking a look at Thailand instead. I know from our people in the United States that you don't agree with us. But they all say that you are honest, that you will write both sides of the story as you see it."

She was an impressive woman. Making a joke of the fact that she was in her late thirties, she told me that she had spent all of her adult life in the Communist Party; she was certain that in the end things would go her way. She spoke openly about her activities as a schoolteacher; when I asked if she indoctrinated her pupils, she said "yes."

My dinner companion's identity is unimportant. The point is that she does exist, that there are scores like her in Thailand. They are neither marauding insurgents ensconced in the mountain jungles or fork-tailed devils racing through the streets of Bangkok, jabbing people with a pitchfork fashioned out of a hammer and sickle. They are, by contrast, the Dorothy Healys of Thailand: perfectly respectable people, excellent neighbors and good dinner companions, who are totally convinced that a Communist or socialist state is the best way of life for their country.

She began, as the Communists always do, with a recitation of the government-caused ills of Thailand. Her indictment is unimpeachable: its bill of particulars runs from poverty to neglect, from exploitation to political tyranny. When I agreed that her indictment was correct but questioned whether one could, in all intellectual honesty, say the government in Bangkok is totally responsible for everything that is wrong in Thailand, she showed fire.

"I'm not stupid," she said in perfect English. "These ills are historical. These moral fools running things in Bangkok did not start all this, they inherited it. What I'm saying is that the government seeks to perpetuate the ills rather than to end them."

The evening started with dinner at Nick's Number One, and ended four hours later in the cocktail lounge of the President Hotel.

Much of what she told me I had already learned from non-Communist sources. But as she developed her arguments she spoke as a devout Communist who approved of the insurgency and looked upon the events that produced the uprising as a kind of spiritual manifest destiny. Although most of her facts were old to me, her flavor and interpretation of these facts was quite new. According to my dinner companion, then:

The Communist Party in Thailand will soon celebrate its fiftieth anniversary. It was formed when a hodgepodge of intellectuals and socialist organizations were pulled together by the "Paris Group" under the leadership of Pridi Phanomyong and Pibul Songram. The spawning ground was Thamasat University, the political science university, set up by Pridi shortly after he returned from Paris and while he held high credentials in the Thai government. The Party's political arm was the Kanarasd, People's Party, which sparked the overthrow of the God-King in 1932. Even after the Communist Party was outlawed, students at Thamasat University continued to carry out Communist dialogue. After all, the students claimed, Communism was a legitimate subject for study and debate in the political science university.

From the outset the Communists concentrated on Bangkok intellectuals, a fertile target because so many of them had been trained in the liberal political atmosphere of Europe. It simply is too much to ask a man who has spent five years in Paris to return home to Thailand and support a God-King. The students from the northeast offered the Communist Party an opportunity to exploit the sectional and class struggles that have beset Siam from its earliest days as a nation. The Bangkok students tended to treat the northeast scholars as unsophisticated country bumpkins. The northeasterners struck back by becoming clannish and by adopting a slogan one Thai intellectual translates as "since we are number two, we try harder." Indeed they did try harder; as a result, northeasterners became the outstanding students at the university. This is the spirit that produced Krons Jandavongs and his daughter Rassamee.

The weakness of the early Thai Communist movement lay in its Moscow orientation and control. During its early years, the Party exhausted every effort, applied every rule of Marxism, in a vain attempt to set off revolts among the students and workers. They simply couldn't get mass support. The philosophical approach was too Russian, and hardly at all Thai. But all this changed in the early sixties. Pridi by then was ensconced in Red China as the Thai government in exile. It is estimated that at least a dozen Thai exiles are now there with him.

Consequently, the Thai Communist movement became Peking-oriented rather than Moscow-oriented. Money, men, and orders began to flow into north and northeast Thailand from southern China. People from Laos and North Viet Nam also began to move into Thailand. And it was with the arrival of these Peking-oriented peoples that the Thai Communist Party completed the switch from Moscow to Peking.

The Thai Communist Party, a small band of intellectuals and public servants, has approximately five thousand active members throughout Siam. My dinner companion, a Maoist, strongly believes that Russia is flirting with capitalism and will one day ally herself with the United States against China. However, according to her, Asian Communism will be strong enough to dissuade Russia and the United States from launching an open conflict against China. Meanwhile, the Thai Communist Party is continuing its work and is actively engaged in recruiting. Party meetings are forbidden, but there is nothing to stop individuals from having dinner together, going to races in small groups, gathering in the plush lounge of the country club to drink. The Western concept of an organization that meets in a hall, that opens every session with the reading of the minutes of the previous meeting and adjourns by passing resounding resolutions in time to meet the early editions of the *New York Times,* is long since outmoded. Rather, four or five people meet for a drink, which is not against the law, and hear that Rassamee or Yod needs, say, mimeograph paper. It is quickly decided who will get the paper and pass it on to a panting courier from the northeast.

The Thai Communist Party is carefully hewing to the Maoist line of organizational development. Mao has written and preached that every "peoples' revolution" must be indigenous; that the people must support the movement with their talents, their money, and their lives. You don't send thousands of Chinese to carry out the overthrow of the Thai government. You do train Thai dissidents, you even give them a few Chinese advisers. But these Thais must return home, live off the land, and raise an army of their own people. The Thai Communist Party is now in the "army-raising" stage. And they are confident that the Thai government will do most of the work for them. The simple faith is that the now-awakening peasants will remember past and present grievances against Bangkok and then ally with the Peking-oriented Lao, North Vietnamese, and Chinese. It is also hoped that by its excesses toward loyal Lao and North Vietnamese in the north and toward loyal Chinese in the south, the Bangkok government will forge a Thailand-wide army of revolutionaries.

"This is why the insurgents have not struck at your

airbases in our country," she said to me. "We could do it any day, any night in the week. But then you would strike with fury and destroy us. One day there will be fifty thousand Communist Thais to contend with—all over Thailand: in the north, the northeast, the south, and here in Bangkok. Your ambassador is right when he tells the press that Thailand will not be another Viet Nam. It will be a hundred times worse!"

"Your Ambassador Graham," she continued, "thinks he can win over the Thai peasants by telling them that the Bangkok government has their concerns at heart. The Thai people have known Prapas and his clique longer than you Americans have; we know what these men are like. Your government will never convince the Thai people that the Bangkok junta loves them. Look at what you are doing," she said, launching into a long denunciation of the work carried on by American AID and Information officers in the back villages. Typical of the programs she excoriated was the one being implemented in south Thailand as we were talking:

Irwin Pernick, a New Yorker and a veteran Foreign Service officer, arrived in Yala with his wife and child. Now on loan to the United States Information Service, Pernick and his wife moved into a Thai house where Mrs. Pernick spends most of her day protecting their daughter from mad dogs and deadly snakes. Pernick spends his day traveling, with Thai allies, into remote villages near the Malay border where they distribute posters and show films depicting the government in Bangkok as "the good guys," the Communists as the "bad guys."

"This approach simply will not work," she said. "The people don't believe in it. Even the sophisticates in Bangkok know that their government is not a 'good guy.' "

Then she discussed the growing unrest among the Chinese, Laotian, and Vietnamese minorities in Thailand.

Again, it was not the newness of the information, but the fact that the Communists are forging their movement out of this unrest that caught my attention.

"The Vietnamese in the north are not free to travel," she reminded me. "They cannot travel from village to village without the approval of the district officer assigned from Bangkok. They cannot have their own schools, nor can they hold meetings. They are not allowed to work at night. Well, this may stop Communists from meeting in the open, but it also stops the Vietnamese Catholics from attending church in the next village on Sunday, and it stops the Vietnamese fishermen from fishing at night on the Mekong when the catch is good. There is nothing your Ambassador Martin can do to turn these peoples toward Bangkok. They have no alternative but to join us."

As she spoke, I remembered what Maynard Parker had written: "This repression [against the Vietnamese] has been confining. It has forced many neutral non-Communist Vietnamese into the hands of the Communist cadres, street committees, assassination squads, and agitprop teams."

Then she spoke of the Laotians, most of whom are deeply Thai. In essence, here is what she said:

There is no question that thousands of pro-Peking Lao for Laos have filtered into Thailand since 1960. It is all but impossible to distinguish a Thai from a Laotian Lao. Had Thailand been a country where people registered and voted, where individuals were citizens with established records and identities, it would then be a simple matter to distinguish a loyal Thai citizen who happens to be of Laotian extraction from a Lao who has crossed the Mekong bent upon subversion. But the Thai citizen is a nonentity, practically ignored by his government. Thus, once he leaves his small village of, say, twenty or thirty families, there is no way of knowing just who he is or where his loyalty lies. The result is that hundreds, and perhaps thousands, of loyal Lao have been arrested and held under the martial law that prevails, often for long periods of time, until they can prove their loyalty.

"This is why we have taken to the back villages," the Thai Communist remarked to me. "For the first time in their history, the lowly peasants are being asked to participate in the coming of a better way of life. Bangkok never did this; they came into the villages and told the peoples what to do. We go into the villages and enlist the peoples' help in doing something for the people themselves.

"Look," she said, pointing out toward the street from the cocktail lounge. "See those poor men driving put-puts [tiny three-wheeled scooter cars that have replaced rickshaws in Bangkok]; they don't own them. They drive day and night, they rent those things from a middleman, a Chinese. These drivers go home with a few bahts a day. They must pay half of that for the put-put. This means the driver is lucky if he makes a dollar a day. Why shouldn't the state own those things? Why should people work to make money for other people? If that man has to rent his put-put, he should be renting it from the state and the rental money should be going to provide better schools, roads, and housing for that man and his family.

"The same applies to the rice farmer," she continued. "He farms the rice, sells it to a Chinese middleman who, in turn, sells it to the government. Why shouldn't the farmer deal with his own government? Why the middleman? If the Chinese want money, let them go out and work for it like everybody else."

It was at this point that I raised the question of anti-Chinese feeling among the Thais.

"I am not a racist," she replied. "This is a class, not a racial conflict. The rich Chinese exploit their own people. This is particularly true in the south. The Chinese peasant is exploited by the Chinese merchant. The Chinese don't discriminate," she added with a touch of flipness; "they exploit Thais, Laotians, Malays—as well as Chinese."

Then she abruptly switched to another subject. "There is something I had made a point of remembering to talk to you about," she said. "You have been asking me about Rassamee. What you seem not to have discovered is that the insurgency movement has an enormous following among Thai women. Rassamee is the glamour figure in the hills, but there are hundreds of Thai women who serve as messengers and supply officers for the insurgency. You should understand this because it is the same thing that has happened to the Negro woman in America. The Thai male has been emasculated, doomed to the rice fields. It is the Thai woman who, as a servant, has seen the better life. She, more than the radio and the television, has taken the gospel of the good life to the peasants. This is why there are so many women involved in the insurgency movement. Thai women are insisting upon a better way of life."

What would the Thai Communist do if a constitution were promulgated, if the people, men and women, were allowed to elect their officials?

"The constitution will come," she replied quickly.

"You Americans will see to that. This is the only way you can save face. But it will be like the constitution you are promulgating in Saigon. The elections will be so staggered that the people will never get a sense of full participation and the electorate will be rigged so that only the pro-Bangkok people will have power. In fact," she continued, "the constitution will create even more dissidents, possible supporters of the insurgency. Bangkok simply is not going to allow the masses to participate in a free and open election. We will find fertile ground among those who are not allowed to vote."

I insisted we return to the question of the minorities in Thailand, only to discover that she regarded the issue as minor.

"Our greatest gains," she interrupted, "have been among the Thai people themselves. The Thais do not have a political commitment, either to Communism or capitalism. Even the Bangkok government is uncommitted. They are reacting to *Chinese militarism, not Chinese Communism.* Had Chiang Kai-shek remained on the Chinese mainland and flexed his military muscles, Russia, not the United States, would be occupying Thailand today."

"But America has occupied us instead," she continued. "You have occupied Thailand and South Viet Nam. Now what are you going to do with us? How long can you continue to spend a billion dollars a month, plus men? Suppose you actually won a military victory in Viet Nam, what would you do with the country? You could turn it over, in name at least, to General Ky! But you would have to occupy the place for twenty-five years to keep the people in line. All of the programs to clean up the poverty and racism that crippled your country would collapse. To put it bluntly," she concluded, "we cannot match American fire power, but we can drive you insane and make you spend yourselves broke."

Are the Thai Communists committed to the violent overthrow of the Bangkok government?

Her reply was pure Marxism: "We don't want violence. But the Bangkok government has, and always will, choke off all nonviolent processes. When there is no legal way for the people to express their will, then they must use illegal methods, usually violent, to get justice. This is the reason for the insurgency.

"Time is on our side," she continued, "there is no reason to hurry. The way and nature of man is against capitalism. People just can't live that way; they will get tired of trying to prove something to you Americans. We understand

Western minds but you do not understand our way of thinking. If an American general were in charge of the Communist insurgents in Thailand, he would have us immediately start a major conflict here; his reasoning would be that this would give America a war on two fronts. This is not the way the Oriental mind functions. It would be much more to our way of thinking to plunge you into a war in Thailand on the day you sign an armistice in Viet Nam."

I came away from the talk with the Thai Communist certain that the Communists are not going to launch a major military campaign in the near future. It was she who gave me the title for this book: Thailand is the war that is, the war that will be.

Since I left Thailand, events have proved her point; there will be a constant campaign of insurgency activity. The Communists will hack away at the back villages, they will deeply infiltrate the dissident Thais, the North Vietnamese, the Lao, and the Chinese in the south against the day when even the most loyal of those peoples will desert Bangkok and join the insurgency.

I rode back to my hotel that night in a put-put, the essence of the interview boiling within me. I had the haunting, sinking feeling that I had heard it all somewhere once before. Then I remembered. Years ago, in New York, I interviewed a man named Fidel Castro.

THE SIX-MILE WALK

It is simply worthless to seek interviews with spokesmen of the Thai government. Not only are they especially apprehensive about foreign newsmen, but when Thai officials do consent to talk, they refuse to say anything that adds substantially to what a journalist can read in the weekly press statement released by Minister Prapas. Perhaps it is too much to expect that a country which has never granted political freedom to its people will embrace the notion of a free and investigative press. An even more modern rendering of the Thai government's position would compare its notions about the press with those of former Assistant Secretary of Defense Arthur Sylvester, who said that the press should serve as the "handmaiden" of the government, that control of the press is one of the weapons in the government's arsenal. It might be recalled that Mr. Sylvester also once said that the government has "a right to lie" in times of crisis.

I am not critical of the Thai government when their censorship of the news is essential to national security. Rather, I speak of the all too frequent instances when the truth is suppressed not for military reasons, but because it might prove politically embarrassing to the government in power. Every dictator has abolished freedom of the press on the grounds that open inquiry and dialogue would endanger the republic. The great fear, of course, is that free discussion might well enlighten the people who, in turn, could bring down the government for malfeasance.

The best evidence is provided by Thai newspapers themselves. The two Thai dailies are rigidly controlled by the government. The two English-language dailies, both foreign-owned, live in fear of being closed down should they stray too far from the government line. As a result, the Thai papers fawn and flourish each day as they give detailed accounts of the goings, comings, and doings of the royal family. There are documented instances in which editors were berated for having failed to carry pictures as well as stories of the activities of the royal ones. When I was in Thailand, not a single Thai reporter was covering the insurgency in the northeast and the south. They sit at their desks and write innocuous little stories about how good things are under the Thanom regime.

This absurd behavior cannot be attributed to concern for national security. I stood with the peasants along dusty roads in the northeast and watched American planes take off. The interested reporter does not have to trouble himself by counting the planes, but only has to make notes of the various types. Hanoi radar tracks every flight involved. One need only tune in Radio Hanoi each night to know precisely how many American planes took off from which airbase. The broadcasts even give the type and the make of the planes, sometimes the serial number. But the no-news nonsense sometimes backfires.

During my lunch with Ambassador Graham Martin, he launched into a quiet tirade about Americans who flit about the world apologizing for their country, for its foreign policy. He told me he was going to strike back in a speech he was soon to deliver before the American Chamber of Commerce in Bangkok. (Bob Beecham, Ambassador Martin's official press chief, missed the lunch because he was busy writing the speech in question.) Shortly after I returned home, Ambassador Martin did indeed make the speech. Not only did he criticize America for self-flagellation but he announced, for the first time, that we were using Thai bases and gave the number of American servicemen based in Thailand. Martin had hardly finished his speech before Minister Prapas called in the press and challenged Martin's figures. In essence Prapas said that if upward of forty thousand American soldiers were in Thailand, the Thai government was unaware of it!

American spokesmen delight in quietly telling reporters that all of the sleight of hand about the news is at the request of the Thai government. That is not the whole truth. American officials have enjoyed the secrecy of the past two years because it muzzled debate back home. It also kept the American people from knowing what their government was doing. The same pattern emerges from Viet Nam. American reporters stood with thousands of Vietnamese and watched as the converted Navy carrier *Core* sailed up the Saigon River and began to unload helicopters and crewmen in front of the Majestic Hotel. When reporters asked for information, the American press officer said, "What carrier in front of the Majestic Hotel? We are not authorized to see any carrier!"

A few days later Radio Hanoi broadcast the exact number of helicopters that had been unloaded, giving airframe and engine serial numbers. As Malcolm Browne, chief Associated Press correspondent for Viet Nam and a 1964 winner of the Pulitzer prize, noted, "The official U.S. attitude was that the public should be kept in the dark even when it was obvious that the enemy had the facts."

I will add the same about our presence in Thailand. The only people who don't know what is going on there are the Americans and the Thai masses. I must belabor this point to make a clear nexus between what occurred in Viet Nam and what is now occurring in Thailand.

The year was 1962. The official American position was that American troops were in Viet Nam to advise the South Vietnamese, but that they were not actually involved in combat. Malcolm Browne visited Da Nang airbase and took pictures of two T-28 two-seater fighter-bombers as they taxied up to the ramp. Their bomb racks were empty, and fresh smoke stains trailed back over the wings from their guns. American security men pounced on Browne and took his film. It was not the T-28s that made the Americans tremble; it was the pilots. Vietnamese pilots were indeed aboard the crafts, but they were sitting in the back seats. The front seats—the command seats from which the bombing and strafing missions were flown—were occupied by Americans. Had Browne's pictures been printed, Americans would have choked on their morning coffee as they gaped at pictures of blond, blue-eyed Vietnamese pilots returning home after having bombed and strafed the Viet Cong. Americans also would have known that their government was lying, that Americans were already fighting and dying in Viet Nam. That was in April of 1962. It wasn't until February of 1965 that the American government officially announced that our men were directly involved in the Vietnamese conflict!

This is 1967. The official line is that our men are in Thailand as advisers, as guests of the Thai government, that they are not directly involved in the deadly hunt for Yod, Rassamee, and their insurgency cohorts. American officials in Bangkok hasten to tell reporters that not a single American has been killed or hurt in Thailand. I don't believe it. Our casualty reports from Southeast Asia are lumped under the Viet Nam war. There is no way of knowing whether a man was killed or injured in Viet Nam, in Thailand, in Laos, or in Cambodia. The truth will emerge when someone comes up with a picture of a peasant stumbling across the body of a dead American in the Thai jungles. Although the Thai insurgents have deliberately avoided violent encounters with American AID and Information workers, they would not hesitate to fire on American pilots ferrying Thai counterinsurgency troops into the jungles.

On a visit to the *New York Times* office in Bangkok I read a wire story out of Washington that said the American government had asked the Thai government for permission to enlarge some of our bases there to accommodate B-52s. This was shocking in light of the fact that neither Washington nor Bangkok had ever admitted that the bases existed. I asked both the Thai and American governments about this request. The Americans said they knew only what they had read on the wire. Bangkok people said it was all in a murky state, that talks were going on between the Thai ambassador in Washington and the State Department. The truth is, and was, that even then the bases were being enlarged. The agreement had long been settled.

Early in March 1967, the two governments reluctantly

confirmed that permission to enlarge the bases had been given. Now the bases are in use. B-52s are being transferred from Guam to Thailand. And we the people are asked to believe that the scheme advanced from agreement to execution in less than sixty days. Not even America can build an airbase with such speed.

These are but some of the reasons why reporters find it futile to spend precious hours with official government representatives. I did go through the motions of seeking a top-level interview while in Thailand. For the record, I proceeded through Bob Beecham, and was told that government officials were too busy to see me. Certain highly placed Thai friends, however, did arrange for me to have a long private walk with a major government spokesman, a man who is completely knowledgeable about both the insurgency and the Thai-American axis.

We quickly dispensed with the nonsense. He confirmed the presence of American bases and estimated that some fifty thousand American soldiers were stationed in Thailand. Yes, the agreement of military assistance was both mutual and irrevocable. It does mean that Americans will fight in Thailand if the need arises. It also means, he added with a smile, that should Canada attack the United States, Thais will help man the ramparts at Detroit.

The Thai government now takes the insurgency seriously. After five years of denying and posturing, even to itself, Bangkok now admits its neglect of the northeast and simultaneously seeks to make amends and stamp out the insurgency. The Thai official questioned the figures I gathered in the northeast concerning the extent of the insurgency. It was his view that fewer than three thousand people are directly involved. He readily admitted, however, that if the small insurgency groups really began to move, they would certainly get support from thousands in the north, the northeast, the south, and in Bangkok as well.

The Thai spokesman seemed less concerned about the Communist insurgents than he was about the American presence—particularly that of Graham Martin—in his country. He cited an incident that occurred in Viet Nam and was the topic of cocktail conversations in Thailand at this time. The matter concerned one La Thanh Nghe who had been elevated to a Cabinet post in the Ky government despite objections from Washington. La Thanh Nghe's record as a double-dealer and black-marketeer goes back to 1965, when the American government charged him with overinvoicing and demanded that the Olin Mathieson Company return a quarter of a million dollars that taxpayers had paid for drugs shipped through Thanh to Viet Nam and Cambodia. Thanh now stands accused of receiving three hundred and fifty thousand dollars in kickbacks from American and West German drug suppliers *since* assuming his Cabinet post in the Ky government.

"I do not condone what Thanh did," the Thai official said, "but every appointment in our government is cleared with Ambassador Martin. A man he does not like could not be promoted to a responsible post in Thailand. Martin runs the Thai government."

As the Thai official continued to detail his dissent, I remembered an incident that had taken place during my lunch with Ambassador Martin. I mentioned to him that I had not been able to get pictures of Rassamee and Yod. The ambassador looked at Marshall Wright and nodded "yes." After the lunch, Marshall made a phone call and such pictures as the Thai government has were delivered by messenger in less than an hour. The Thai official who was walking with me along the klongs of Bangkok could not have gotten them so quickly, if at all. He knew it, and that was precisely his point.

"We have been an independent people all of our history," the Thai said to me. "We have become an

American colony and I don't like it. The Thai people don't like it. I cringe when I see Thai girls prostituting themselves for American soldiers. It is such a blatant and open thing. I cringe when I see American soldiers swaggering down the streets of Bangkok. Even the Japanese didn't do that. But we cannot help ourselves. We are caught in the hot war between East and West.

"On the other hand," he continued, "what if open elections, free politics that would allow parties to field candidates, produced an anti-American candidate? We cannot say we are going to have national elections and then deny those who don't want Thailand involved in the Viet Nam war to field candidates. That would be a farce, worse than having no elections at all. Your CIA is already active, gathering information on potential candidates. You did the same thing when Sarit came to power. Perhaps one day the American people will know how deeply Thais resent interference in Thai political matters.

"Yes," the Thai commented, "the Thais want political freedom. Beneath the surface freedom there is great unrest." Then he went on to recount an incident that had occurred at a football game a few days before our talk. The Thai cheerleaders had fashioned their placards to spell out an inquiry as to the date of the new constitution. The matter was done with delightful innocence and amid much cheering. But government officials got the message. The Thai students want to vote.

"Of course," the Thai said in response to my question, "the baht is sound. It has to be sound because of the American aid that flows in every year. Our government treasury is solvent. The trouble with bahts," he added, "is that so few Thais have any of them. The greatest economic asset Thailand has is the fact that practically all Thai farmers own their farms. We are not faced with the problem of land distribution that plagues Viet Nam. Our Achilles heel is neglect and poverty in the northeast, racial and religious hatred in the south. This takes us back to the question of the proposed constitution. If we allow universal suffrage, Thailand may well break up along sectional lines. The peoples of the northeast and of the south would vote for secession from Bangkok if allowed to. This has been true throughout our history. Popular suffrage would give us the identical problems that Nigeria now faces. Thai nationalism is as delicately balanced as the spokes of a wheel. That balance must be maintained if the nation is to remain intact."

The Thai official exuded a quiet confidence that Thailand would overcome, that it would not explode into another Viet Nam. "Thailand can work itself out of this situation—if the Americans allow us," he said. "We know our problems, we are awake to them, we can solve them if America helps us. But if America attempts to control us, if we must make Thai interests identical with American interests, then we will have grave difficulty."

Even in anonymity the Thai spokesman was guarding his words. He was articulating an argument I had heard from several Thai intellectuals. In essence it is this: Thailand has maintained its independence because it has always been able to maneuver; to take sides without making long-range commitments; to trade off, as in the case of the Japanese, a military presence in return for noninvolvement. This is no longer true. America has Thailand hogtied. Not only do we base our aircraft there, but we are perched, ready to oppose any Thais who seriously threaten Bangkok. Moreover, the American presence has ended all hope that the Thais could arrive at some kind of détente with their neighbors—the Lao, the Cambodians, and the North Vietnamese—once hostilities end. Also, it is an accepted fact that when the United States moves out of Viet Nam it will come into Thailand and squat near Red China. This means an American occupation of Thailand for the next twenty-five years.

Indeed, we have a renewable fifteen-year lease on our Thai airbases. There are those Thai politicians who are anxious to run on a platform that would politely ask the United States to leave their country. That would bring on a dispute about treaty keeping; but with American bombs falling in Cambodia and American planes flying over Laos, we have long since eschewed our moral position in Southeast Asia. If we flatly refuse to go at the request of an elected Thai government, we would prove to be the big white bully the Asians suspect we are and the Communists would then gather the strength they need to turn the current insurgency into a full-scale war—a war, like the one in Viet Nam, we cannot win.

As our talk neared a close, the Thai official made it clear to me that there was deep concern within the Bangkok government over the activities of American Special Forces such as the ex-FBI men, who are training Thais for counterinsurgency activity, and the CIA. The fear is that these Americans will flex their muscles if and when there are elections in Thailand. Then the Thai dropped a bombshell. "Did you know that a contingent of your Green Berets is now at work in Thailand?"

I was stunned, even though a few weeks before, a former member of the Green Berets had appeared as a guest on my television program and detailed such Beret activities as plotting and executing the overthrow of foreign governments. "No," I replied, "I didn't know that."

"They are here," he assured me. "They are training counterinsurgents. But what else are they doing?"

I returned to my hotel, reminded once again that Thailand is a deeply troubled country. The land of Siam is having dangerous growing pains and America has made an irrevocable commitment in a nation lurching with suppressed internal turmoil.

I went through the motions of calling Bob Beecham and asking if the Green Berets were in Thailand. He assured me that they were not. I didn't believe him. The Thai official was in a position to know; there was no reason for him to tell a gratuitous lie. That was early in January 1967.

Early in March the American government admitted that the Green Berets had been in Thailand since October 1966. Not only are they training Thai counterinsurgents, but only a decision by Defense Secretary Robert McNamara himself kept them from actively engaging in hand-to-hand combat against the Communists in the jungles of Thailand.

The delay in getting the truth out of Thailand now seems to have been cut to six months. Perhaps by the time this is in print we will have accounts of the first American casualties in the mountains of northeast Thailand.

THE FIFTEEN-MINUTE INTERVIEW

Liang Chaiyakarn is one of Thailand's best-known politicians. Now a Bangkok lawyer, he was the beloved member of parliament from the northeast during the days of representative government in Thailand. He received me graciously and promised to talk as much as the law would allow.

Question: Do you plan to run for office once the constitution is promulgated?

Answer: Yes. I am very anxious to run. I will stand for my old seat from the northeast.

Question: When do you think Thailand will have a constitution?

Answer: There is no way of knowing. I have friends high in government and they say we should have a constitution in about a year.

Question: What do you think about the Communist insurgency in Thailand?

Answer: I cannot speak of that matter.

Question: Do you think your government is taking adequate measures to arrest the insurgency?

Answer: I cannot speak of that. The law does not allow it.

Question: What do you think of the American presence in Thailand?

Answer: I cannot speak of that. The law does not allow it.

Question: What matters can you address yourself to?

Answer: Other than to say I hope to run for office, I cannot speak. The law does not allow it.

Question: Can you exert any effort toward getting a constitution for Thailand?

Answer: No. I must be silent and wait. I have friends who are in a position to work for a constitution. Once it is promulgated, I can announce my candidacy.

Question: Is that all you can do?

Answer: Yes. I can only sit and wait.

Question: Is there any more you can say as of now?

Answer: No. The law does not allow it. But please give my regards to the people of America. I was there as a guest of President Eisenhower. You have a wonderful country.

The interview was over.

THE TIES THAT BIND

Thailand, in more than just geography, is a sprawling country. The proud and wealthy Chinese hotel owner in downtown Bangkok makes the rice peasant from a northeast rice field appear to be an aborigine; yet they are both Thais. The Thai speaking the central Thai language of Bangkok makes one question whether or not the man speaking Thai-Malay comes from the same planet; yet they are both Thais. The sophisticated Thai woman who dresses in the latest Paris fashion to attend a royal ball does not impress one as the sister of the wrinkle-faced old woman whose arthritic fingers paddle a leaky boat along the klong that parallels Freedom Road; yet they are sisters, they are both Thais. The obviously white woman who is the cashier at the Bangkok Hotel stood chattering away with the almost black woman who was the desk clerk. The conversation was about the love mishaps of the distinctly brown woman who worked as director of the hotel's cleaning staff. They all laughed with great abandon and understanding. They are all Thais. The Moslem removing his shoes to enter the Temple of Yala and the Buddhist walking barefoot into the Temple of the Emerald Buddha in Bangkok are both Thais. The Communist who joined me at dinner, the government official who walked with me along the klongs, the Thai intellectual who argued that democracy was only for the educated elite, the mayor of Nakornpanom who called Bangkok officials "bastards," the Lao who runs the barbecue-chicken place along Freedom Road, the Phu Thai who come down from the mountains to fish—they are all Thais. Rassamee and Yod, along with their followers in the mountain jungles, are Thais also.

What, then, keeps Thailand together?

There are those who argue, and with much correctness, that Thailand is not really a nation; that it is still a group of city-states, kept together by fear of Bangkok and mysticism about the Great Lord Buddha. These Thai observers believe that Thailand will fly apart one day, when the right sectional and factional buttons are pushed. Others argue that Thailand is a nation, that its strength lies in its diversity. Those of this view go on to say that the God-King image is the Thai universe, that all Thai peoples will respond cohesively should a moment of great crisis arise. Their contention is that the Communist insurgency is just the thing Thailand needed to achieve true nationalism and complete unity. Their opponents maintain that the insurgency is just the thing that will cause Thailand to fly apart.

Whatever the truth, the question of Thailand's stability as a nation, as host for America's all-out effort against Asian Communism, must be thoroughly examined.

Because the village is the prime social and political unit in Thailand an examination of intervillage relations and the ties of the villages to Bangkok will provide some assessment of overall stability in Thailand.

I have already written that the Thai village is an enclave of poverty and neglect. The people live simply, in small communities that seldom exceed a hundred families. They work hard, farming rice or whatever crops grow well in their particular area. The center of village life is likely to be the Buddhist temple. Once upon a time—and this was true for centuries—the temple was also the center of education. This is still true in some of the remote villages. The curriculum is, of course, theology-centered. Nowadays, however, the village youth who attends school migrates temporarily to the nearest urban center.

At first glance one would think that village life is sedentary, that the life of the villager is one long yawn, an unending bore. Yet the contrary is true. In reality, village life is a beehive of unending activity. What we must not do is impose Western standards of measurement on these peoples. The Thai villagers are, on the whole, adjusted to village life; it meets their needs as they see them. The villager does not want to be uprooted and transplanted to Bangkok. He wants Bangkok to aid him in his endless efforts to better his own village. If Bangkok cannot mount a sincere effort to help improve conditions, then the villagers wish Bangkok would withdraw its meddling policemen and local officials.

In the past decade, two developments have given Thai village life a new energy and infused a sense of rising expectations. The first was the impact of Western culture and technology, particularly farming implements; the second, the American presence. The District of Chiengkham provides an excellent case in point.

According to Professor Michael Moerman, who lived in the District of Chiengkham for two years, there was not a single wheeled vehicle there thirty years ago. Today, most of Chiengkham farms are plowed by hired tractors. This has brought about a tremendous change in village life. In the past, village families lived a communal life in the long house. They all worked together in the fields while the long-house elders provided the basic subsistence for the young couples, who, in turn, were expected to clear new fields and buy additional land of their own. The rice gathered from the long house went into the community larder, while the grain gathered from newly cleared land provided the "private rice" with which couples were expected to set out on their own.

So laborious and slow was rice farming, however, that couples were seldom able to strike out for themselves until they were middle aged and their children were married. The tractor changed all this.

Today's village youths are able to acquire considerable land and private rice even before they are married. Once married, they are able to build homes for their families. The back villages of Thailand are now dotted with young, independent households. But serious cleavages have been created between the young and the old in the Thai village. As Moerman points out, only men younger than thirty-five have worked as soldiers or teachers for the national government. Only women younger than thirty have gone to school, only girls younger than twenty have grown up regarding the milling machine as a normal convenience of daily life. Shades of Marxism! Mechanization has indeed produced class conflict. But the young Thai still has deep reverence for his parents, disputes are still settled by ancient tribal codes of justice. But the tractor is not the only significant Western gadget to have an influence upon Thai village life.

Moerman and his wife lived in a village where there was only one shop. It was owned by a Chinese. Mrs. Moerman tells of going shopping and finding the store stocked with packets of cigarettes which were made in Thailand, but patterned after American brands. There were also cans of sweetened or condensed milk imported from Holland or Denmark. Moerman says that most of the villagers bought these Western items but they did not use them. Rather, these items were taken to the temple as an expression of village piety.

What impressed me most about the villages I visited was the constant interchange of goods and other items from one household to another. Everybody had something to trade off, but there was no exchange of money. Sharing one's goods with others is a form of Thai brotherhood and tribal fidelity. I came away with the distinct impression that here was a very sophisticated form of communal living. I doubt that records show a single instance of starvation in a Thai village. It simply couldn't happen. The people are totally involved with one another.

Whatever happens to one happens to all. The worst thing that could happen would be a flood that destroys the rice crop. Floods have occurred and entire villages have faced economic disaster. But it was not an individual matter.

Village male youths have great mobility and they must not be compared to the European serfs who were tied to their land. These fellows, almost all of them, leave home in their mid-teens. Some of them join the priesthood and wander the length of Thailand, dressed in their holy robes and sandals. They live off the earth and get to know the people. The begging bowl is their symbol. The majority just move around. Their great joy consists of traveling from town to town, village to village, getting to know the peoples, and, all the while, deflowering maidens along their path. Most of them wind up in Bangkok where they find some kind of work and build a nest egg. Most of them come back home, marry and settle down to live, eventually to die.

Thai village women do their share of wandering too. Some of them go off to school at the nearest big town. They too come home to live and to die. Most of the Thai village women have been to the market, along Freedom Road, in Nakornpanom and Bangkok. They also come back home to live and to die. The point I am stressing is that the Thai villager today is not a stupid, isolated child of the earth. He has seen and heard the offerings of a general world society deeply at odds with itself. The old villager who, after two years, thought Moerman and his wife came from Ceylon, the land of the Buddhist scriptures, must be compared to the old Negro who lives on the plantation in Mississippi still trying to adjust to the liberalism expressed in the Emancipation Proclamation.

The second impact on Thai village life is the American presence. There is not a day when the back villagers do not see American helicopters flying over their heads, that they do not hear the drone of American jet bombers. And when they come to the main village to market their grain, they see the American soldiers swaggering down the dusty roads, they see the Thai police scrambling aboard a helicopter to launch yet another search for Rassamee and Yod. And, by night, followers of Rassamee and Yod are apt to descend upon villages, spout Communism for four hours, demand rice, and then vanish into the jungles. They may not understand the abstract political and economic issues that undergird the conflict, but the villagers know they are caught in a war to the death between two forces.

The question finally becomes whether the structure of modern Thai village life bodes well for national unity in

Thailand. Were Bangkok's traditional neglect of the villages still the order of the day, one could easily conclude that the Communists will win. That, however, is no longer true. Thus, we must stay a conclusion until we examine what Bangkok—with Washington's help—is doing in the villages and assess its impact.

Two incidents—one described by Professor Michael Moerman, the other by Maynard Parker—aid greatly in this analysis.

Thailand, through the Minister of Interior, has launched a major program "to encourage the people to exercise initiative, to improve their communities and way of life through cooperative efforts on a self-help basis." The United Nations adviser suggested that the best way to get this idea implemented would be to have monthly meetings in each district. According to Moerman, who attended such a meeting in Chiengkham, this is what took place.

The meeting of November 20, 1960, was extremely elaborate. Headmen had been told to arrive in uniform at 8:30 in the morning so that they would have time to rehearse their welcome to the provincial governor, who was expected at 10:00 A.M. The district's schoolteachers had made a huge banner bearing the legend, "Meeting for the Primary Demonstration of Community Development. First Time: 2503 B.E. *Amphur* Chiengkham." This was the first indication the headmen were given that the meeting concerned community development. On the stage which the district officer and other high officials would occupy were a microphone, a phonograph, a Buddha altar, and placards, some in Thai and some in English, illustrating poverty, ignorance, malnutrition, and disease. Although the governor never arrived, these stage properties showed the solemnity and importance of the meeting.

The district officer read for over an hour from a mimeographed address sent him by a superior official in charge of community development. He emphasized and added to those parts of the address which interested him most. Thus, for example, he quickly read through the qualities of the good local leader of community development and stressed the need for getting rid of bad leaders. He spent little time on the need to foster expressions of local opinion, but elaborated upon the elimination of gambling, repairing roads, keeping villages orderly, and, of course, building toilets. He announced which villages had been chosen for development and ordered its headmen to make sure that these things were done by the time a community development official arrived from the provincial capital the following year.

Throughout his assigned address the district officer managed to communicate his faintly puzzled amusement at each reference to the need for community initiative. At one point in his talk he contrasted the villagers' old attitude of respectful fear toward the officials with the desired new spirit of intimate friendship between them. Here the district officer and his audience burst into laughter, no longer able to contain their amusement at such strange ideas. After lunch the meeting reconvened for the formation of small discussion groups of teachers and headmen. Each group was to select one of five major problems of community development, discuss it, and report back to the entire meeting. For the most part, only the teachers were active in these groups. The headmen and other villagers sat quietly and spoke only when directly questioned. When a show of hands was called for, they first looked to see how the others were voting, perhaps thinking as they raised their hands, let's do what the majority want. The public reports given by the teacher-spokesman after the discussions were recapitulations of the speeches made earlier by the district officer and other officials. At the end of the meeting the district officer announced that all in attendance had been chosen as local leaders of community development, and would therefore be required to give a voluntary contribution of thirty bahts to the Red Cross.

Clearly, this meeting for Primary Demonstration in *Amphur* Chiengkham was quite inconsistent with the philosophy of self-help and local initiative. The rehearsal for the governor (who did not appear), the failure to announce the purpose of the meeting, the labor exacted from the teachers, the incomprehensible signs in English, the air of authoritarianism, the emphasis on command, punishment, and conscription—all this set a tone hardly in keeping with the abstract rules of community development.

Some will counter that this was mainly true in 1960, during the early days of the village experiments, but surveys conducted in late 1966 revealed little appreciable change. It was disclosed that community development workers arrived in northeast villages selected for model-village experiments and set about their work much as an engineer in battle goes about building field fortifications. Not only did the workers fail to consult the villagers about needed programs, but the people soon discovered that their villages had been taken over by workers who could not speak the local dialect. Land was taken to build roads —without the consent of the owners; Bangkok directed workers to build new toilets—but they went unused because there was no water to operate them with. Yet the toilets are still being built—along the main road, in full view of visiting supervisors from Bangkok. One wonders if it occurred to the community development workers that a peasant needs his toilet at his house, in the small trees, where he can use it; and that he needs water to make the contraption function. The community development workers are not concerned about making things convenient for the villagers; their goal is a promotion, an ambition that cannot be fulfilled unless the visiting supervisor from Bangkok can see the shiny new toilets as he motors down the main road—which is about as close as he will get to the back villages.

Maynard Parker visited the model village of Ban Papark late in 1966. The village is situated some thirty miles from the Mekong River border with Laos. (It will be recalled that this is the same village the Communists struck when I was in northeast Thailand.)

> "After leaving the main road," Parker wrote, "I walked for an hour over a muddy trail, past high teak trees and rice paddies streaked with crevices from lack of rain. It was startling to come on a sign rising out of the midst of this jungle which read, 'Welcome to the CDW.' As I walked into the village, welcomed by the usual barking of village dogs, I passed a neatly fenced plot with a sign in Thai designating it as Sample Farm Number One. Inside the fence a mass of weeds strangled out any plants which might have grown there. Obviously no one had cultivated the sample farm in months. I was given a tour of the village by its aging headman, Suan Songsri. He showed me the four existing wells, Ban Papark's only water supply. In each, the water was as dark as chocolate and bugs puckered its surface. Suan had tried three times to build a dam near the village for irrigation, but each time the dam had washed out in the rainy season. A district officer had given him cement to build another dam, but since the villagers lacked sufficient engineering skill, it too had washed away.
>
> "This lack of water was painfully apparent. In the fields the rice was brown, the ground was cracked. No vegetables or fruit could be grown in the village, and so the children's bellies were swollen with malnutrition.
>
> "Suan did not look like a leader. Barefoot, deep brown from the sun, his only garment was a purple *pakoma,* a Thai sarong. He had attended school for only four years and had never ventured twenty miles from his village. He had married twice and had fourteen living children. Yet as we walked down the streets, the

villagers greeted him respectfully, bowing their heads very low and raising their palms pressed together to their faces—the traditional Thai greeting. By Bangkok's standards he was a simple peasant, yet he knew far better than Bangkok officials what his village needed. He was far more respected than they by his villagers. He was a valuable man for the government, but Bangkok chose to ignore him, and in so doing, negated much of the good work they had labored so furiously to build."

The Communists are convinced that the current flurry to aid the peoples in the south and the northeast is so much toilet-by-the-main-road activity. They are not the only ones who take this view. Maynard Parker says that the Bangkok-appointed civilian police in the remote areas have been "more effective in irritating local officials than in rounding up Communists." My own observations in Thailand caution me to stop just short of that conclusion. Obliquely, I would suggest that the mounting village assassinations have caused local officers and police to become anti-Communist, in behavior, to preserve their lives. By the same token, and for the identical reason, thousands of villagers have joined the Communists. They too want to live.

What I saw in the villages was a combination of the Moerman and Parker reports. The impact of modernism has generated great expectations among the villagers. The Thai and American governments are frantically trying to repent their old sins and create new images.

It simply hasn't worked. American workers scurry around with a guidebook called *Lessons Learned in Viet Nam.* But it hasn't worked there either. The back villagers in Viet Nam still are not loyal to Saigon. There is not enough grain in the American aid program to convince the Viet Nam villagers that Premier Ky loves them. In a move of desperation in 1967—and just before elections—

the State Department backed Ky in the thoroughly socialist move to redistribute upward of three million acres of land. This, of course, is precisely what the Viet Cong have promised to do once they come to power.

The same must bluntly be said of Thailand. The American taxpayers dumped forty-three million dollars into Thailand in 1966. Much of this money went into community development programs in Thai villages. But, as I shall later detail, it didn't quite get to the villagers. Thai district and village officials are notoriously proud and stubborn. When American aides nudge them, the Thais tend to get bogged down in paper work and meetings. It must also be remembered that Thai district officers are afraid to go into the deep back villages. They certainly will not stay there overnight. Thus the promise exceeds the fulfillment. At night the Communists exploit the vacuum. The millions America is spending attempting to portray the Bangkok government as a "good guy" are undoubtedly wasted.

The modern Thai village is a divisive, rather than a cohesive, force for nationalism.

Buddhism is the national religion of Thailand and many view it as *the* great force for Thai nationalism. But one has only to recall the critical situation in the south. The Thai government would guarantee full-scale insurgency in the south, if it invoked Buddhism as the raison d'être of Thailand. This is precisely what the Communist insurgents are itching for. The peoples in the south are almost solidly Moslem, and unlike the Lao of the northeast who eschew the makeshift country that is now Laos, they yearn for unification with Malaya. The fetching young Thai lady who operates the jewelry shop in my hotel begins each day by kneeling before the Buddhist shrine in the hotel courtyard. But her nationalistic challenge, at least in part, is to work out an accommodation with the equally fetching young Thai lady who works in a jewelry shop in Betong. She interrupts each day's work to turn eastward and cry aloud to Allah.

But there is something much more disturbing—as we discovered in Viet Nam—about suggesting that Buddhism is a national force that binds Thailand. It rips the Moslems from the Thai mainstream and ignores the mounting expectations among the devoutly Buddhist masses. Even more, as orthodox Christianity did in America, Establishment Buddhists in Thailand are shielding the ruling powers from the reality of discontent in Thailand.

Like Christianity, Buddhism is otherworldly. We Negroes of the Deep South have a saying: "Prayer is fine in a prayer meeting, but it ain't worth a damn in bear meeting." Of course we are talking about our encounters with the Southern white man. The only way we could pray our way out of the hell that was Birmingham, Alabama, was to send our prayers aloft while we sat in the streets and blocked off traffic. Not only did God get our message, but United States Steel, whose plant we all shut down, got the message as well. Now Negroes eat where they please, use the bathroom at the nearest place whenever they feel the urge. They go to the polls freely. This would not have happened had prayer remained a Shakespearean closet drama acted out in some dilapidated church building.

Buddhism, by the same token, is a spiritual closet drama. It does not evidence an economic or social commitment until earthly gripes erupt into a near riot and disturb the Establishment. Then, and only then, do the deeply religious announce that God—the Great Lord Buddha—is on their side.

Buddhism, as a religious movement, ails from the same affliction that crippled Christianity and that produced

Malcolm Boyd, Bishop James Pike, and Malcolm X. Christianity could not accomplish the social reform demanded by some of its adherents: it could not get them changed. Father Malcolm Boyd took to the night clubs to relate Jesus to the teeny-boppers, Bishop Pike faced charges of heresy because he came on my television program—among other places—to say that he was not concerned about Mary's virginity but he was concerned about world brotherhood; and Minister Malcolm X left the Baptist Church in order to announce that all white men were devils. The whole world remembers Hitler's acid remark that the Pope didn't have enough divisions to get anything accomplished on this earth.

Buddhism in Thailand is still at the stage of telling its adherents that should they live the good life, they will be better and wiser in the next world. But as Viet Nam proved, a powerful Buddhist leader can emerge and translate all this into immediate social action. Alas, there is not a single leader within the Buddhist Establishment in Thailand who can do this. Like the Catholic bishop in Havana who bows to Castro, the Buddhist hierarchy fawns at the Royal Palace in Bangkok. They acquiesce in the Bangkok government's cumulative sins.

Little wonder, then, that the majority of peasant Buddhists are waiting for Pee Boon, the delivering Messiah.

The ultimate concern of every organization is self-perpetuation. If the organization is religious, then its ultimate concern is to establish God as they see him. This keeps the bahts coming, and it also keeps the leaders in power over their flock. Once the government allows them to exist—this is particularly true if they represent the majority of the peoples—the religious leaders staunchly support the status quo. Thus the Temple ceases to reflect the concerns of the people and becomes an arm of the government. The rising expectations of the masses are scorned by their own religious leaders. Only Pee Boon makes sense any longer.

I have no alternative but to view Buddhism as a divisive, not a cohesive, force in the spectrum of Thai nationalism.

Thai schools are organized in a tidy fashion, and it is not difficult to view the Thai educational system as binding all Thailand in cohesive nationalism. After all, as M. L. Manich Jumsai concludes in his excellent UNESCO study, few nations of the world have as centralized an educational system as Thailand's. All schoolteachers are national employees; they work for the Ministry of Education in Bangkok. The teacher wears the khaki uniform that distinguishes all Thai officials; his status is determined by civil service gradations which are paralleled in all other branches of government. Everything—salaries, textbooks, promotions, educational policy, budgets, standards of instruction as well as examinations—is determined in Bangkok. Thai schoolteachers are public servants in the ultimate sense of that term. They serve under the authority of the district officer and can be required to perform any task the government desires.

The Thai teacher lives closer to the farmer than most Thai officials, yet his commitment to Bangkok exceeds that of any headman or district officer. The teacher is Bangkok's ambassador to the village. He brings with him the national language, Bangkok Thai. Teachers from the villages in the north, the northeast, and the south often complain that beginning students have difficulty understanding simple commands, such as "close the door," when these orders are issued in Bangkok Thai. Required by law to employ Bangkok Thai, teachers accomplish their task by teaching it as a mandatory second language.

The object of Thai education is to instill strong feelings of nationalism. Pupils are drilled in the history of the nation and are taught to worship its heroes. Morality is equated with Thai Buddhism and civics classes stress loyalty to Thai officials, and above all, to the king.

The failure of Thai education, as I see it, lies precisely in its rigidity, in its nationwide chanting of a daily paean to Bangkok. True, the system now assures that at least one person in the remotest of back villages can speak Bangkok Thai. But it has also resulted in young village Thais being urged to worship a government they neither understand nor respect. Equally fallacious is the assumption that if all Thai youngsters are taught to speak the national dialect they will rally around Bangkok. Common language does not constitute common commitment and rote utterances of loyalty will not satisfy the growling bellies and curious minds created by the worldwide tide of rising expectations.

But the schoolteachers are there, in the villages. Their presence is not to be regarded lightly. The teacher epitomizes Bangkok's authority over, rather than involvement with, the village. He comes as an order giver rather than as a problem solver. This is why the teacher is a prime target when the insurgents come into the village by night. There is little that the teacher says or does that alters the basic fact of a village-oriented life. The teacher may bring Bangkok to the villages, but he fails to involve the villagers with Bangkok. The Thai national government is an uninvited, not a welcome, guest in the village. This is why all the headmen laughed when the district officer orated about closer cooperation between district and village officials. Until this image of Bangkok is changed, I cannot view Thai education as a force of national unity in the remote areas far to the north and south of Bangkok. And the image cannot be refurbished by slapping picture posters of Bangkok officials on village trees and inside village toilets. Such "good guy" posters make excellent dart targets, but they are hardly calculated to engender instant nationalism.

Yet another insight into why Thai education fails to inculcate nationalism can be gained by examining the current behavior of hundreds of teachers in the remote areas. I spent an evening with a group of American Peace Corps workers in northeast Thailand. One of them told of an escalating and disturbing development. He was so determined that his message be heard, that I found a moving letter from him waiting for me when I returned to Los Angeles. The Peace Corps worker wrote, in part:

> When you write about what you saw in Thailand, I hope you include for ALL [capitals are his] to read that there are some of us who actually cry when we see what the United States Military Policy is doing to this country. Tell them about all the Thai teachers who leave their schools to become interpreters and clerks at our military bases at three times their original salaries. Tell them about the Thai agriculturalists who desert their experimental stations, who desert their work with the farmers, to work at our military bases. Their job is "to make the base beautiful and pleasant to the eyes." They now get five times their original salary. Tell them about the Thai engineers who leave their road-, dam-, and bridge-construction jobs to build runways and supply houses for our military bases. They now earn seven times their original salaries.
>
> Tell them, tell them . . .

In the parlance of American hustle it is quite the accepted thing to leave one job and take another to make more money. But in the eyes of a young American who has interrupted his studies to go to Thailand out of a spiritual desire to help the Thai people, and is actually living on peanuts and rice, this behavior is sheer sedition. It certainly makes the point that Bangkok's ambassadors to the back villages lack commitment. Teaching school is much more dignified than threshing rice; by the same token, a high-paying job around free-spending Americans can be utopia for a graduate of one of Thailand's teachers colleges. But what is the Thai villager to think when the local teacher leaves her pupils to work at an American airbase? He doesn't have to ponder the question very long. At night, Rassamee and her followers sweep down into the villages with a ready answer: *Bangkok doesn't give a damn about you; the teacher doesn't give a damn about you, he only wants to make money without hard work. The Americans have taken over our country.*

The painful truth is that Rassamee is correct. Even more painful is the fact that Rassamee would stay with the villagers, teach them, live with them in the rice swamps, if the Thai police and the American helicopters weren't interfering. Rassamee and Yod's teaching would emphasize ideas, not the worship of Bangkok. Most of all, Yod and Rassamee believe so deeply in their idea that they are willing to lay down their lives to bring about its fruition. By contrast, the schoolteachers showed what they believed in when they left the schoolhouse to work at the American airbase.

But, I suppose this is too much to ask of peoples whose educational system prepares them to stand in unison and sing "All Hail Bangkok."

The American embassy in Bangkok eagerly distributes fact sheets on the king. An excerpt from a bulletin issued by His Majesty's Private Secretary reads:

> His Majesty King Bhumipol Adulyadej of Thailand was born in Cambridge, Massachusetts, U. S. A., on Monday 5th, December 1927, being the youngest son and third child of Their Royal Highness Prince and Princess Mahidol of Songkhla. Since His Royal Highness Prince Mahidol was a son of His Majesty the late

King Chulalongkorn, His Majesty is therefore a direct descendant of the great monarch.

His Majesty was at Mater Dei School and later proceeded to Lausanne, Switzerland, for His further education. After finishing His secondary education, His Majesty studied science. Circumstances, however, compelled Him to change His subject of study. His Royal Brother, His Majesty King Ananda Mahidol, who succeeded to the Throne in March 1935, died unexpectedly in June 1946. His Majesty succeeded Him as the 9th King of the House of Chakri. In order to prepare Himself for the function of kingship, His Majesty went back to Switzerland to study political science and law. In April 1950 His Majesty married Queen Sirikit. He came back to this country for the Coronation, which took place on the 5th May 1950. He then went back to Switzerland to continue His study, but before he completed His course of study, the call of his country and the pressing need of His people made Him return definitely to this country in 1951, and He has been residing here ever since.

Honestly translated, this says that the present king's brother was found dead in his bed, a bullet between his eyes; that the good King Bhumipol was plucked out of school in Switzerland by the military plotters and set upon the throne to keep the masses in mysticism.

There can be no doubt, however, that the king is the most beloved man in Thailand. He is adulated for both his ancestry and his much publicized Buddhist piety. King Bhumipol is a most likable fellow and his activities make excellent fairyland copy for Thai newspapers. The king blows a smooth saxophone and the word is that he actually keeps the ruling military junta from excessive excesses. But, alas, the king is a nobody when it comes to influencing government policy.

Once upon a time, the king could have unified Thailand. Now it is too late, much too late. The military have destroyed his divinity and the intellectuals have destroyed his authenticity. The masses, on the other hand, have enjoyed his existence. He is their Linus blanket, something to snuggle with when the cold winds blow. The king can no longer unify Thailand. The peoples in the south want out. The peoples in the northeast don't want Bangkok in. King Bhumipol cannot change this.

I am not suggesting for one moment that Thailand is going to fly apart. It will not. But one day, like the one-horse shay, it will fall apart. Whatever nationalistic glue there was is now as dry and crumbly as it was spurious. And America's presence is not going to save the day. This is Thai nationalism's seminal hour, but the motherland does not have the political health to give birth to a stable new government.

What Thailand lacks is political commitment. A series of governments—from the God-King to the present military junta—have reigned without the cooperation of the people. With American know-how we could feed every man and woman in Thailand. Even if we assigned a spit-and-polish Thai official to bring in the food—and we will—the peasant will not turn toward Bangkok and genuflect. Once his belly is full, the Thai-Malay, if allowed, will vote to join Malaya. I tremble to hazard a guess as to what the northeast Thais would do if Rassamee and Yod were allowed to run in an open election. The one thing I do know, and I do not hesitate to say it, is that they would not vote for Bangkok. They would seek an alternative.

THE NIGHT WE RODE THE ELEPHANT

One reads that America will spend a hundred million dollars in Thailand during 1967; that upward of fifty thousand American servicemen are stationed in the land of Siam; that some two thousand American civil servants are laboring there as Peace Corps workers and as Information and AID officers. These cold figures give the flavor of our involvement. But the impact is not truly felt until these figures take on flesh and blood, until one sees and hears what they feel and think.

A dozen of us gathered in a Thai house, high on stilts,

in Nakornpanom. It was a party for Americans only. We had come to ride the Thai Elephant. Everybody—the Peace Corps, the Air Force, the Army, the United States Information Service, the United States Operation Mission —was there. Excellent steaks, somehow obtained from the American airbase nearby, were also there. But what brought us together was the promise of a ride on the Elephant.

It is like drinking lukewarm coffee. The Elephant had been conceived and brought to a fermented state in a huge ten-gallon earthen jar. First, the jar had been filled to the three-fourths mark with sticky rice. The rice was then overlaid with a mixture of rice husks and a yeast peculiar to Thailand. Finally, the jar was filled with water, covered with a wooden top, and planted six feet in the Thai earth to work its magic wonders.

Six weeks later, unearthed and bubbling fumes, the Elephant sat in the middle of the room. The tusk, a long reed one-half inch in diameter, was shoved midway into the jar. To take a ride, one sucked Elephant juice through the reed until the water level disappeared beneath the husk. As applause and cheers rang to the ceiling, the host added water to the Elephant for the next partygoer to demonstrate his powers. After we all had taken three rides on the Elephant, the party started.

We were a gathering of loud and joyous brooders. In an exercise of group therapy, people started getting things off their minds. A Peace Corps worker was the first to really feel the Elephant's strong kick. When we became aware, he was sitting alone crying. It was new for me, but the others had lived through such sessions before. It's one way Americans working in the remote areas of Thailand stave off insanity.

"Why did they send the goddamn Army in here?" he sobbed. "We could have done it!"

The soliloquy came from a twenty-three-year-old American who had joined the Peace Corps with stars in his eyes. He wanted to help America save mankind from hunger and ignorance. He had really dug into his village assignment. The villagers were digging wells, making roads, building toilets. He was teaching their children to speak English. Most of all, he had presented a picture of America as a land of growth and progress, a place where people tackled their problems in a civilized manner.

Yes, of course, he knew about the insurgents. They had come near his village, but Rassamee and Yod had not bothered the American. The real burden that beset the Peace Corps fellow was that his method had failed. He had honestly believed that education and community development would save the Thai villagers to themselves and from Communism. He expected to accomplish the miracle without a shootout in the jungles. Now all that is dream stuff. Even as we rode the Elephant, helicopters and jets droned overhead.

Nancy, his date for the evening, was also a Peace Corpsman. A schoolteacher in Nakornpanom, she lives in a rickety Thai house behind the school with several Thai schoolteachers. Nancy is a very lonely American missionary.

The Thai schoolteachers keep to themselves. The American does not feel completely accepted. She brooded about what was going on back home at the University of Wisconsin, wondering if she was missing anything. Most of all, Nancy pondered whether her sacrifice had been in vain. Whatever hope she had—that the Peace Corps would allow her to do creative work among the underdeveloped—has long since been destroyed by the rote and routine nature of the Thai educational system. Nancy was hurt because the Thai teachers seemed to lack dedication. While she worked with Thai children for a pittance, Thai teachers were defecting to the military bases for higher salaries.

The two Peace Corps workers snuggled up together and comforted each other.

"If you want to talk to a 'round eye' (an American girl) call this number when you get back to Bangkok," the airman said as he handed me his card. The "round eye" was his wife. He flies missions over Viet Nam three weeks a month and then takes a week's vacation. Somehow his wife and three children just happened to take an extended trip from St. Louis, Missouri, to Bangkok where she rents a house. Dependents of the U.S. military are not allowed in Thailand, but visitors are. So, when her visitor's visa expires, she simply flies north into Laos and returns to Bangkok with a new visa.

"I wonder if what we are doing in Viet Nam is getting results?" he brooded.

His monologue was that of a man carrying out an assignment he does not completely believe in. He seriously questioned the thesis that America can bomb Hanoi into peace talks. He revealed deep-seated doubts about the morality of America's involvement. But he was Air Force to the core. He did say to me that the Air Force had just "pulled the smartest goddamn trick ever on the Viet Cong." He apologized for not being able to tell me about it. But he wanted us to share his pride in the Air Force.

Pride was indeed in order. Two days before we rode the Elephant, he had participated in a raid over North Viet Nam in which American pilots lured a fourth of the North Vietnamese air force to its death by camouflaging fighter jets to make them appear as reconnaissance planes on the Hanoi radar. That was great fun.

The pilot was, by far, the life of the party. He and I made a pact to collaborate on a book about his war experiences when he completes his twenty-year hitch in early 1968. It should be quite a book, particularly the chapter that will detail how he flew a small plane over

Laos and guided the returning bombers to the point where they jettisoned their excess bombs.

The old man of the party was a construction engineer in his mid-fifties. He and his wife have tramped the earth building roads and airfields. New roads in Viet Nam bear his trademark. He had only recently come to work in Thailand.

"I would still be in Viet Nam," he said, "if we hadn't bombed those three villages by mistake."

"Were you in the villages?"

"Hell yes. I was working on a road in the area and saw our planes bomb all three of those villages by mistake. I grabbed a jeep and raced into the center of the village near where I was working. It was just awful. I saw too many dead people whom I knew and worked with. I had to leave," he concluded as he took another ride on the Elephant.

The United States Information Service man was a very quiet and correct civil servant. Though friendly, he smiled slowly. His conversation was less brooding and more a matter-of-fact admission of the way things are.

The USIS, which is chartered by Congress to disseminate information about the United States in the remote areas of the world, has been transformed in Thailand into the propaganda arm of the Thai government. Several times a month this USIS official and his Thai employees go on field trips into the back villages. They show films and pass out literature deliberately designed to give Bangkok the "good guy" image. The pretense is over. The notion that the purpose of the USIS is to inform people in Thailand about America is openly scoffed at. Ambassador Graham Martin has barked the orders and the entire American Information and AID program in Thailand is devoted to the propagation of the current Thai regime.

Thai broadcasting, both radio and television, has been

taken over by American AID and Information officers. Many hundreds of Americans labor in cramped offices of a downtown Bangkok building, turning out radio and television programs designed to transmute the ruling junta into the Trinity of Southeast Asia. The programs are well done, yet the message is as blatant as any paid political ad. The Thai listeners and viewers are never told that this is propaganda, that the program has been written by Americans, that its basic purpose is to sell Bangkok. Like the word of God, these broadcasts simply come through the air on the wings of omnipotence for the people to hear and obey.

"Can you, in good conscience, tell the Thai villagers that Bangkok is a 'good guy'?"

"Look," the USIS officer fired back at me, "I don't construct the USIS program. The program is laid out in Bangkok and Washington. I am told to carry it out. If this is what we have to do to fight Communism, then this is what we have to do. It doesn't make sense to spend American taxpayers' money to tell Thais about George Washington and the New Deal when Rassamee and Yod are running free in the hills. We have to counteract Communist propaganda. Granted, Bangkok is far from a free democracy, but it is the only non-Communist crap game in the country."

"And we are rolling craps for airbases," the pilot interrupted. "Seven come eleven. Daddy needs a new landing strip."

Shortly before midnight, those of us who had managed to survive the Elephant ride went into town for a midnight snack. Nakornpanom was bulging with the military. The voices of America—the shouts of poor Southern whites and Negroes—crackled through the air:

"Now boy, you pedal this three-wheeled rickshaw fast; you hear?"

"Yaaahooo! I wish I was in Dixie!"

"Did you hear what that peckerwood mother said?"

"Watch out for that Thai whore in the red dress. She is a mean one. Last week one of our boys told her she wanted too much money and she whipped out a knife and cut off her own right thumb. Scared the shit out of everybody."

"Lordy, Lord! When we got about fifty miles from Hanoi this morning, the SAMA were so thick you could gather them like eggs. Those Russian missiles sure can fly high. I sure was glad when the captain ordered us to drop our load and haul ass out of there."

"*You,* Lomax? I heard you debate Malcolm X in Cleveland. You cats sure told it like it was."

"Professor J. L. Lomax your daddy? Man that cat was my school principal. Ain't this a bitch. We meet in a Thailand shit house!"

It was as if all mankind was on an eternal Elephant ride. Good and evil canceled each other out and the line between sanity and insanity is called "duty." I went to my hotel in hope of a long sleep. It was not to be. For early morning was the time when things went "boom!" When the earth shook and the tables rattled.

THE WASHINGTON-BANGKOK AXIS

Today it is Viet Nam, tomorrow it will be Thailand. Today's debate rages around the historical facts of our involvement with Saigon. Who invited us there? When were we invited to take up arms against the Viet Cong? Why were we invited? Were we invited at all, or is the Viet Nam conflict a war of our own making? Could it possibly be that we, America, are the aggressor? What is the legal basis of our commitment to South Viet Nam? How do we morally defend our actions before the world, to ourselves?

Tomorrow's debate will rage around our commitment to

—and in—Thailand. Who involved us with Bangkok, and why? Upon what legal and moral basis do we defend our participation in the search for Rassamee and Yod? What is the truth about the Washington-Bangkok axis?

Not even the Congress of the United States knows the full facts about our alliance with Thailand. During the summer of 1966, Senators J. William Fulbright and Wayne Morse asked for hearings on Thailand, but the Johnson Administration flatly refused to allow open testimony before the Senate Foreign Relations Committee. William Bundy, Assistant Secretary of State for Asian Affairs, did agree to testify behind closed doors. Neither Fulbright nor Morse was convinced by what Bundy told the committee.

"Mr. Bundy didn't tell us anything the nation had not already read in the newspapers," Senator Morse complained.

Fulbright had an even stronger reaction. On October 3, 1966, Fulbright took to the Senate floor to make the speech that was to totally rupture his long, close relationship with Lyndon Johnson.

"We are building up in Thailand," Fulbright told his colleagues. "We are building barracks, airbases, ports and supply depots. What are the reasons for this new military involvement in Southeast Asia? What is the legal basis and the political justification? Are we trying to apply the lessons learned in Viet Nam, are we falling into the same errors or are the two situations not analogous? We are building up in Thailand," he concluded, "but do we know *what* is building up in Thailand?"

These are disturbing questions, particularly since they are raised by the chairman of the Senate Foreign Relations Committee. Clearly this republic has been committed to yet another war without the advice and consent of the people. Pressed for information William Bundy said:

"Well, we have a treaty relationship with Thailand, of course, in that they are a member of the SEATO treaty [the Southeast Asia Treaty Organization]. We have a fully complete treaty relationship there. Now that applies to action in accordance with our constitutional processes in the event of external aggression and for consultation in the event of subversion. What you have now is some kind of—well—a real threat of insurgency, particularly in the northeast area of Thailand."

Early in 1967, Senator Robert Kennedy elected to press the issue. I called the New York senator and asked if he would provide me with a copy of the agreement that allows America to use Thai airbases. "We are certain no such written agreement exists," the senator's press aide said. "It all seems to be based on a handshake agreement between Washington and Bangkok." I then called Oscar Armstrong, chief press officer for the State Department's Asian section, and asked for the agreement. Mr. Armstrong said that there is no such document, that the entire arrangement is being carried out under the articles of the SEATO agreement.

What does this mean? No one who has studied the SEATO agreement could conclude that it authorizes our use of Thai airbases, that it justifies our involvement in Thai counterinsurgency. Late in the fall of 1966 the Fulbright Committee asked Arthur Sylvester, Assistant Secretary of Defense for Public Affairs, to clear up the mystery of the Washington-Bangkok axis. This climactic exchange occurred between Senator Fulbright and Mr. Sylvester:

FULBRIGHT: You do not like to talk about Thailand. I am very curious about Thailand. In fact, we have asked your Defense Department to come up and testify about Thailand. I assume you know that they are very reluctant to do it in public sessions at this time. You know that, do you not?

SYLVESTER: Yes, I am aware of that.

FULBRIGHT: Have you been advised not to testify about it also?

SYLVESTER: No, I have not been advised. My own good judgment, knowing what the situation is, which I am sure you know also, would suggest to me to ask you not to ask me that in public.

FULBRIGHT: You see, this is what presents me with a great dilemma. I feel that I was led into the Tonkin Gulf Resolution [the Senate resolution that gave Lyndon Johnson a free hand to escalate the war in Viet Nam] and I have only myself to blame for it because I should have been more intelligent, more far-seeing, more suspicious, but I was not and I fell for it. Now we are faced with what looks like a repetition—by that I mean —faced with a *fait accompli,* a situation that we have to take. Certainly this committee is not created to be a rubber stamp. This is why I want to know what the Administration has in mind in Thailand; that is all. It is just that simple. Are we going to have another Viet Nam there? I think we are entitled to know it. Do you think that is an unreasonable attitude on the part of a senator?

SYLVESTER: Not in the least. On the contrary, I concur completely.

FULBRIGHT: Obviously we are having some difficulty.

The difficulty, of course, was a total breakdown of communication between the military and the Congress. The same breakdown exists between the Johnson Administration and the people. The hard facts concerning our involvement in Thailand simply do not exist in written form—at least not in a document available to the people and their elected representatives. Whatever truth can be pieced together requires that we recall the era of 1954. It was during that year that Secretary of State John Foster Dulles, a devout Christian completely committed to the theology of Americanism, arranged a meeting of Asian and South Pacific states, along with England and France, in the hope that a mutual defense treaty could be struck. It is naïve, to say the least, to suppose that Dulles' main concern was with the involved nations themselves—that, say, New Zealand needed protection against Australia. The object of the conference was containment of Red China—and all of the participating nations well knew it. The Indian and Indonesian delegates listened to the proposal and then opted out. Eight nations—the United States, France, England, Australia, the Philippines, Pakistan, New Zealand, and Thailand—remained and signed the Southeast Asia Collective Defense Treaty. Manila was host to the conference and Bangkok became the home of the treaty organization.

A clear hint of what was to come lay in the opening paragraph of the treaty, in which all nations reaffirmed their faith in the United Nations. Had this been true, one wonders why it was necessary to go outside the United Nations and form an additional peacekeeping organization. The question was hardly worth asking since Americans had already formed NATO, a European line of defense against Russia, clearly outside the United Nations. Even State Department officials admit that Dulles was motivated by a fear that the United Nations could not move with the military swiftness and political expediency necessary to head off a Communist takeover. But the United States was not the only nation that had an axe to grind outside the United Nations.

Britain was at the conference, in 1954, because she wanted protection for her colonial interests in Malaya; France agreed to the Manila document in the hope that she could maintain control of Laos and Viet Nam; Pakistan agreed because she shares a border with Red China. (Ironically, India refused to join SEATO precisely because Pakistan was a member.) The Philippines were having trouble with the Red Huks, but in 1954, the Philippines were, as they are now, military allies of the United States; Australia and New Zealand, both white and loathed by yellow Asians, were there to protect their borders and reaffirm their oneness with the United States. Thailand, of course, was anxious to join SEATO as a protection against Red China, and to placate the United States as well.

Much of this has already been undone. Britain has lost Malaysia; France no longer occupies Laos or Viet Nam. Our European allies remained in SEATO, however, but their main role seems to have been to frustrate American foreign and military policy. Long before France began to boycott SEATO, the American government had decided to discuss its military plans for Southeast Asia in private with friendly Asian nations. Such matters were never discussed in formal SEATO meetings during the last days of French membership. "After all," one American said to me, "telling the French what you plan to do is the same as telling Hanoi and Peking!"

The same is suspected of Pakistan. World diplomats are convinced that she traded SEATO secrets in return for sporadic periods of friendship and trade with Red China.

Early in 1962 both Thailand and the United States agreed that SEATO was an ineffective organization. In March of that year Secretary of State Dean Rusk and Foreign Minister Thanat Khoman of Thailand issued a joint memorandum that became the basis of the Washington-Bangkok axis. Few members of Congress are aware of the document, although it is the subject of a State Department press release dated March 6, 1962. The wording is more ambiguous than that of most such documents, yet the memorandum clearly states these facts:

1. The United States and Thailand agreed that Article II of the SEATO treaty allows them to make a bilateral agreement that will then become binding upon all members of the treaty organization.
2. The two governments then agreed to make whatever

private pacts they felt were needed to stop Communist aggression. This is justified under Article IV of the SEATO treaty.

3. The United States also agreed to defend Thailand against direct or indirect aggression.

The entire document is concerned with providing security for the government in Bangkok. Not one word in the memorandum relates to the question of Thai bases being used by American aircraft as a point from which they can bomb North Viet Nam. On the contrary, the memorandum suggests that American military men are in Thailand to protect that country. An official document issued by our embassy in Bangkok says that we are developing Thai airbases in order to "modernize and enlarge Thailand's military and logistical facilities."

That allegation is totally untrue. America is determined to menace whatever it deems to be Communist in Southeast Asia and we have committed ourselves to defend any government, regardless of how corrupt and wrong it may be, that allows us to use its territory as a convenient base from which to carry on our anti-Communist activity. Similarly, the Rusk-Thanat Memorandum is a spurious document; it involves SEATO far beyond the consent of the member nations; it makes an interpretation of the SEATO agreement which is not supported by the letter of that treaty; most of all, it is, in effect, a murky, handshake understanding between the Johnson Administration and the current Bangkok government. The terms, length, and conditions of that understanding are not known. The Washington-Bangkok axis is, in all practical terms, an illegal treaty. It has never been ratified by Congress.

Today SEATO, as a result of American unilateral action, is in shambles. The April 1967 meeting of the treaty organization was little more than a sophisticated brawl. France wouldn't attend; Pakistan refused to send its

Foreign Minister and the Pakistani ambassador to Washington sat in on the meeting instead. Even before the meeting began Australia and Thailand attacked Britain, France, and Pakistan for "enjoying all the privileges of SEATO membership without accepting any of the responsibilities." South Viet Nam—not a SEATO member—came as an observer and her delegate applauded as the conferees agreed to support the American position in Viet Nam. But Pakistan refused to be identified with the motion to support America, and Britain voted "yes" only after the motion had been rewritten. According to British Foreign Secretary George Brown, the original declaration of support contained "too much talk of war, too little talk of peace."

War, even more than politics, makes for unlikely bedfellows. The Washington-Bangkok axis is being strengthened, not weakened. American military and economic involvement in Thailand is being increased daily and the capacity of American-occupied Thai airbases is constantly being enlarged. Thai officials have threatened to restrict American military personnel to their bases because prostitution in Thailand is undergoing an unprecedented boom. And American officials have refused to sign a "status of forces" agreement that would subject American soldiers to Thai law—because they do not respect the Thai courts. In Thailand people are tied to the stake and shot after the most perfunctory trial procedure. America is not willing to have its servicemen tried under such procedures. And this, perhaps, is the most telling comment that can be made about the Washington-Bangkok axis: Americans are committed to die in defense of a government whose laws are so unjust that the American government will not allow Thailand jurisdiction over American soldiers who walk and yell along the streets of Bangkok, Nakornpanom, and Udorn. Little wonder the Thai peasant of the northeast and the south smiles in his rice when he sees posters saying the government in Bangkok is a "good guy."

This, I fear, is going to be the pattern followed by both Washington and Bangkok for as long as possible. They will either stand silent or issue murky comments about the insurgency in Thailand. Not until the ultimate accident occurs, until an American dies in the jungles of Thailand in so flagrant a fashion that we cannot tell his family that he died in Viet Nam, will the people hear the truth about our obligations under the Rusk-Thanat Memorandum. That day may not be too far away. Late in April of 1967 the Thai police overran an insurgency camp and discovered documents which prove that the insurgents have rescinded their "hands off" policy toward American servicemen. Leaflets signed by a group calling itself "Thais who love their country" offer a five hundred dollar bounty to any Thai who assassinates an American serviceman based in either central or southern Thailand. Identical leaflets have been circulated among the peasants in the northeast, but the bounty is not quite so high. Two hundred dollars is being offered for the assassination of a flying officer, one hundred dollars for a ground officer, and fifty dollars for each enlisted man slain. A close Thai friend has informed me that the insurgents have moved to take over the brothels in towns near American airbases.*

The Washington-Bangkok axis must soon face the moment of total public exposure. Even now nerves are severely frayed and strained. Foreign Minister Thanat Khoman followed up his CBS television appearance by issuing an angry blast at Secretary of State Dean Rusk. "Thailand did not ask for secrecy about the airbases," Thanat charged. "The American government imposed

* As of July 1967, American soldiers on leave from Viet Nam are being sent to Australia rather than to Thailand for relaxation. The Thai government requested the action because of "the rise of prostitution and the decline of Thai morality." However, it is clear that both the Thai and American governments are deeply concerned about possible assassinations.

the news blackout. Now Washington is trying to pass the buck to us. We didn't do it; they did!"

Three weeks later Paul Sithi-Amnuai, Vice President of the Bangkok, Ltd., stunned an audience of American scholars who specialize in Thailand by delivering a totalitarian defense of the current Thai government. "True," Sithi-Amnuai replied in answer to a paper I had read, "I cannot vote in Thailand. But my government does provide me the right to cash my checks and travel. I would rather be a nonvoter in prosperous Thailand than a voter who shares in the poverty of India."

During a sharp exchange with me, Mr. Sithi-Amnuai said the American public had no right to know about their government's quiet arrangements with Thailand; he even went so far as to say that Americans should seriously examine that clause in their constitution which gives them the right to know what their government is doing. The reserved anthropologists, economists, and political scientists, who just hours before thought me to be an alarmist, lost their scholarly composure. They joined me in demanding to know the exact terms of the American lease on Thai airbases.

"The Thai government," Mr. Sithi-Amnuai informed us, "is acting out of self-interest. That is the whole of the matter. If the world political climate changes, then we in Thailand reserve the right to change our position. As for the airbases, you Americans are in Thailand at our pleasure. If we say 'Yankee go home,' then Yankee, you go home!"

"What if you say 'Yankee come back?' " I asked.

"Then," our Thai conferee replied with a smile, "Yankee, you come back."

Paul Sithi-Amnuai was reflecting the edginess that has developed now that pointed questions about the alliance are being raised. Nerves are particularly raw in Bangkok where the Thai government has launched an all-out campaign to prove to its peoples that Thailand has not become an American colony.

"We prefer our own Thai way," strongman General Prapas snapped late in May 1967 as newsmen questioned him about American military activity against the insurgents in the northeast. "I still feel confident that it is not too heavy a task for us to cope with ourselves."

Perhaps General Prapas honestly believes the Thai army can handle the insurgency; or perhaps he issues such statements to bolster Thai morale. In any case, it is a grim parallel indeed that America began to entertain open discussion of the failure of the South Vietnamese on the battlefield just as reports from Thailand began to question the aggressiveness of the Thai army. The most shocking reports have come from Sakolnakorn where the third regiment of the first battalion of the Thai army is stationed. Local Thai officials bitterly charge that the third regiment flatly refused to respond to the call for help against guerrilla attacks in the spring of 1967 because the monsoon season had set in. This raised the question of whether American men should be called upon to defend a people who refuse to go out into the rain and defend themselves.

After investing more than six hundred million dollars in the Thai army since 1950, American military officers now flatly admit that the Thai forces lack training, organization, and leadership. Aside from a few military men who were involved in the Korean War from 1951 to 1953, none of the Thai military officers have seen actual combat. However, many have been involved in the periodic palace coups that have plagued Thailand since 1932. The current Thai cabinet, the heads of major government bureaus, as well as the leaders of Thai industry and commerce are military men. They are products of a system in which army service is the path to political power and financial comfort, not to military glory. This is why a military desk job in Bangkok is favored over a unit commandership in the northeast.

This is the way things are in Thailand; this is the "Thai way" General Prapas spoke of when he said Thailand would fight the insurgency on her own. But what if the "Thai way" fails? Then, in Lyndon Johnson's words, "American boys must go and do for Asian boys that which Asian boys should be doing for themselves." But, as the Jack Foise incident demonstrated, the public will need reliable information to provide explanations when our men begin to come home from Siam in pine boxes. Against the day when the great debate over Thailand erupts—and it will—we must list the hard facts we know to be true:

• We know the current Thai government is a tyrannical military junta.

• We know the Thai peoples do not have a constitution; they cannot vote. They have lived under martial law for more than a decade.

• We know indigenous Communist insurgents are operating in the northeast and the south under the leadership of Thais trained in North Viet Nam and China.

• We know that Thai intellectual and military strength is being drained off into counterinsurgency activity.

• We know that Secretary of State Dean Rusk and Thailand's Foreign Minister, Thanat Khoman, formulated a 1962 interpretation of the 1954 SEATO agreement which, at least so the two countries claim, gives them the right to act bilaterally and to carry out military maneuvers they feel are needed to stop either indirect or direct Communist attacks.

• We know that the details of this 1962 memorandum are not spelled out. We know that the legal and moral basis for America's use of Thai airfields, as well as for America's involvement against the Thai insurgents, is not set forth in the Rusk-Thanat document.

• We know that America is bombing North Viet Nam from Thai airbases.

• We know that some American forces are training Thais for counterinsurgency and that other Americans are ferrying Thai troops into the mountainous jungles to flush out the Communists.*

• We know American AID and Information Services officers have been transmuted into propaganda agents for the Bangkok government.

• We know Americans are committed to die, if necessary, to defend the Thai government.

These are facts about which there can be no debate. But in the heat of the war that will be in Thailand all this truth will melt. Passion alone will prevail; reason will have been destroyed by diplomatic blunders. There will be a national clamor to support our men in Thailand, to bomb Red China and get it over with. We will be told that it is better to stop the Communists at the Gulf of Siam than on the shores of southern California. Civil rights leaders will be excoriated because they argue that they cannot get on with their job so long as the Republic is involved in an unjustified war. A splendidly medaled general will come home and go before a Joint Session of Congress in a futile effort to rally the nation.

But there will be a major difference in the Thailand war. Some verdict will have to come in from Viet Nam. America will have lost—lost because a military victory there would be our greatest defeat; lost because a negotiated settlement will give us less than we already have: we will have lost because we never should have been there. We went into the Philippines in the late 1800s, ignoring Kipling's warning:

---

* After training at an air force base in Texas, Thai pilots took over the helicopter operation in June 1967. Americans are still there as advisers.

Take up the White Man's burden
And reap his old reward:
The blame of those ye better,
The hate of those ye guard.

Even now there is great troubling of the national will. And when the Viet Nam conflict comes to an awkward end there will inevitably be a reassessment of our foreign policy. The liberals will become the isolationists, the conservatives will turn into globalists in their relentless pursuit of Communism. Most of all there will be the issue of Americans dying and killing for unclear reasons. The Washington-Bangkok axis is a nefarious alliance and the Rusk-Thanat Memorandum that undergirds it is an exercise in diplomatic treachery. If allowed to work its will, this alliance, this memorandum, dooms us to both internal and international disaster. But if the Congress and the people rise as one and cry "Halt!" to the military-industrial complex, those men of war Dwight Eisenhower so passionately warned us against, then American men will no longer die in the wrong place, for the wrong reasons, and at the wrong time.

THE SOUTH-EAST ASIA COLLECTIVE DEFENCE TREATY

The Parties to this Treaty,

Recognizing the sovereign equality of all the Parties,

Reiterating their faith in the purposes and principles set forth in the Charter of the United Nations and their desire to live in peace with all peoples and all Governments,

Reaffirming that, in accordance with the Charter of the United Nations, they uphold the principle of equal rights and self-determination of peoples, and declaring that they will earnestly strive by every peaceful means to promote self-government and to secure the independence of all countries whose peoples desire it and are able to undertake its responsibilities,

Desiring to strengthen the fabric of peace and freedom and to uphold the principles of democracy, individual liberty and the rule of law, and to promote the economic well-being and development of all peoples in the Treaty Area,

Intending to declare publicly and formally their sense of unity, so that any potential aggressor will appreciate that the Parties stand together in the area, and

Desiring further to coordinate their efforts for collective defence for the preservation of peace and security,

Therefore agree as follows:

ARTICLE I

The Parties undertake, as set forth in the Charter of the United Nations, to settle any international dispute in which they may be involved by peaceful means in such a manner that international peace and security and justice are not endangered, and to refrain in their international relations from the threat or use of force in any manner inconsistent with the purposes of the United Nations.

ARTICLE II

In order more effectively to achieve the objectives of this Treaty, the Parties, separately and jointly, by means of continuous and effective self-help and mutual aid will maintain and develop their individual and collective capacity to resist armed attack and to prevent and counter subversive activities directed from without against their territorial integrity and political stability.

ARTICLE III

The Parties undertake to strengthen their free institutions and to cooperate with one another in the further development of economic measures, including technical assistance, designed both to promote economic progress and social well-being and to further the individual and collective efforts of governments toward these ends.

ARTICLE IV

1. Each Party recognizes that aggression by means of armed attack in the Treaty Area against any of the Parties or against any State or territory which the Parties by unanimous agreement may hereafter designate, would endanger its own peace and safety, and agrees that it will in that event act to meet the common danger in accordance with its constitutional processes. Measures taken

under this paragraph shall be immediately reported to the Security Council of the United Nations.

2. If, in the opinion of any of the Parties, the inviolability or the integrity of the territory or the sovereignty or political independence of any Party in the Treaty Area or of any other State or territory to which the provisions of paragraph 1 of this Article from time to time apply is threatened in any way other than by armed attack or is affected or threatened by any fact or situation which might endanger the peace of the area, the Parties shall consult immediately in order to agree on the measures which should be taken for the common defence.

3. It is understood that no action on the territory of any State designated by unanimous agreement under paragraph 1 of this Article or on any territory so designated shall be taken except at the invitation or with consent of the government concerned.

ARTICLE V

The Parties hereby establish a Council, on which each of them shall be represented, to consider matters concerning the implementation of this Treaty. The Council shall provide for consultation with regard to military and any other planning as the situation obtaining in the Treaty Area may from time to time require. The Council shall be so organized as to be able to meet at any time.

ARTICLE VI

This Treaty does not affect and shall not be interpreted as affecting in any way the rights and obligations of any of the Parties under the Charter of the United Nations or the responsibility of the United Nations for maintenance of international peace and security. Each Party declares that none of the international engagements now in force between it and any other of the Parties or any third party is in conflict with the provisions of this Treaty, and undertakes not to enter into any international engagement in conflict with this Treaty.

ARTICLE VII

Any other State in a position to further the objectives of this Treaty and to contribute to the security of the area may, by unanimous agreement of the Parties, be invited to accede to this Treaty. Any State so invited may become a Party to the Treaty by depositing its instrument of accession with the Government of the Republic of the Philippines. The Government of the Republic of the Philippines shall inform each of the Parties of the deposit of each such instrument of accession.

ARTICLE VIII

As used in this Treaty, the "Treaty Area" is the general area of South-East Asia, including also the entire territories of the Asian Parties, and the general area of the South-West Pacific not including the Pacific area north of 21 degrees 30 minutes north latitude. The Parties may, by unanimous agreement, amend this Article to include within the Treaty Area the territory of any State acceding to this Treaty in accordance with Article VII or otherwise to change the Treaty Area.

ARTICLE IX

1. This Treaty shall be deposited in the archives of the Government of the Republic of the Philippines. Duly certified copies thereof shall be transmitted by that Government to the other signatories.

2. The Treaty shall be ratified and its provisions carried out by the Parties in accordance with their respective constitutional processes. The instruments of ratification shall be deposited as soon as possible with the Government of the Republic of the Philippines, which shall notify all of the other signatories of such deposit.

3. The Treaty shall enter into force between the States which have ratified it as soon as the instruments of ratification of a majority of the signatories shall have been deposited, and shall come into effect with respect to each

other State on the date of the deposit of its instrument of ratification.

ARTICLE X

This Treaty shall remain in force indefinitely, but any Party may cease to be a Party one year after its notice of denunciation has been given to the Government of the Republic of the Philippines, which shall inform the Governments of the other Parties of the deposit of each notice of denunciation.

ARTICLE XI

The English text of this Treaty is binding on the Parties, but when the Parties have agreed to the French text thereof and have so notified the Government of the Republic of the Philippines, the French text shall be equally authentic and binding on the Parties.

UNDERSTANDING OF THE UNITED STATES OF AMERICA

The United States of America in executing the present Treaty does so with the understanding that its recognition of the effect of aggression and armed attack and its agreement with reference thereto in Article IV, paragraph 1, apply only to Communist aggression but affirms that in the event of other aggression or armed attack it will consult under the provisions of Article IV, paragraph 2.

In witness whereof, the undersigned Plenipotentiaries have signed this Treaty.

Done at Manila, this eighth day of September, 1954.*

---

* Signed for Australia by Richard G. Casey, Minister of External Affairs; for France by Guy La Chambre, Minister of State; for New Zealand by T. Clifton Webb, Minister of External Affairs; for Pakistan by Chaudhri Muhammad Zafrulla Khan, Foreign Minister; for the Re-

public of the Philippines by Carlos P. Garcia, Vice President and Secretary of Foreign Affairs, Francisco A. Delgado, Chairman of the Senate Committee on Foreign Relations, Senator Tomas L. Cabili, Senator Lorenzo M. Tanada, and Representative Cornelio T. Villareal; for Thailand by Prince Wan Waithayakon Krommun Naradhip Bongsprabandh, Minister of Foreign Affairs; for the United Kingdom by the Marquess of Reading, Minister of State; and for the United States by John Foster Dulles, Secretary of State, Senator H. Alexander Smith, and Senator Michael J. Mansfield.

PROTOCOL TO THE SOUTH-EAST ASIA COLLECTIVE DEFENCE TREATY

Designation of states and territory as to which provisions of Article IV and Article III are to be applicable:

The Parties to the South-East Asia Collective Defence Treaty unanimously designate for the purposes of Article IV of the Treaty the States of Cambodia and Laos and the free territory under the jurisdiction of the State of Vietnam.

The Parties further agree that the above mentioned states and territory shall be eligible in respect of the economic measures contemplated by Article III.

This Protocol shall enter into force simultaneously with the coming into force of the Treaty.

In witness whereof, the undersigned Plenipotentiaries have signed this Protocol to the South-East Asia Collective Defence Treaty.

Done at Manila, this eighth day of September, 1954.

THE PACIFIC CHARTER

The delegates of Australia, France, New Zealand, Pakistan, the Republic of the Philippines, the Kingdom of Thailand, the United Kingdom of Great Britain and Northern Ireland, the United States of America:

Desiring to establish a firm basis for common action to maintain peace and security in South-East Asia and the South-West Pacific;

Convinced that common action to this end, in order to be worthy and effective, must be inspired by the highest principles of justice and liberty;

Do hereby proclaim:

First, in accordance with the provisions of the United Nations Charter, they uphold the principle of equal rights and self-determination of peoples and they will earnestly strive by every peaceful means to promote self-government and to secure the independence of all countries whose peoples desire it and are able to undertake its responsibilities;

Second, they are each prepared to continue taking effective practical measures to ensure conditions favourable to the orderly achievement of the foregoing purposes in accordance with their constitutional procedures;

Third, they will continue to cooperate in the economic, social and cultural fields in order to promote higher living standards, economic progress and social well-being in this region;

Fourth, as declared in the South-East Asia Collective Defence Treaty, they are determined to prevent or counter by appropriate means any attempt in the Treaty Area to subvert their freedom or to destroy their sovereignty or territorial integrity.

Proclaimed at Manila, this eighth day of September, 1954.

APPENDIX B / DEPARTMENT OF STATE FOR THE PRESS
MARCH 6, 1962/NO. 145

THE RUSK-THANAT MEMORANDUM

Following is the text of a joint statement by Foreign Minister Thanat Khoman of Thailand, and Secretary of State Dean Rusk:

The Foreign Minister of Thailand, Thanat Khoman, and the Secretary of State Dean Rusk met on several occasions during the past few days for discussions on the current situation in Southeast Asia, the Southeast Asia Collective Defense Treaty and the security of Thailand.

The Secretary of State reaffirmed that the United States regards the preservation of the independence and integrity of Thailand as vital to the national interest of the United States and to world peace. He expressed the firm intention of the United States to aid Thailand, its ally and historic friend, in resisting Communist aggression and subversion.

The Foreign Minister and the Secretary of State reviewed the close association of Thailand and the United States in the Southeast Asia Collective Defense Treaty and agreed that such association is an effective deterrent to direct Communist aggression against Thailand. They agreed that the Treaty provides the basis for the signatories collectively to assist Thailand in case of Communist armed attack against that country. The Secretary of State assured the Foreign Minister that in the event of such aggression, the United States intends to give full effect to its obligations under the Treaty to act to meet the common danger in accordance with its constitutional processes. The Secretary of State reaffirmed that this obligation of the

United States does not depend upon the prior agreement of all other parties to the Treaty, since this Treaty obligation is individual as well as collective.

In reviewing measures to meet indirect aggression, the Secretary of State stated that the United States regards its commitments to Thailand under the Southeast Asia Collective Defense Treaty and under its bilateral economic and military assistance agreements with Thailand as providing an important basis for United States actions to help Thailand meet indirect aggression. In this connection the Secretary reviewed with the Foreign Minister the actions being taken by the United States to assist the Republic of Viet-Nam to meet the threat of indirect aggression.

The Foreign Minister assured the Secretary of State of the determination of the Government of Thailand to meet the threat of indirect aggression by pursuing vigorously measures for the economic and social welfare and the safety of its people.

The situation in Laos was reviewed in detail and full agreement was reached on the necessity for the stability of Southeast Asia, of achieving a free, independent and truly neutral Laos.

The Foreign Minister and the Secretary of State reviewed the mutual efforts of their governments to increase the capabilities and readiness of the Thai armed forces to defend the Kingdom. They noted also that the United States is making a significant contribution to this effort and that the United States intends to accelerate future deliveries to the greatest extent possible. The Secretary and the Foreign Minister also took note of the work of the Joint Thai-United States Committee which has been established in Bangkok to assure effective cooperation in social, economic and military measures to increase Thailand's national capabilities. They agreed that this Joint Committee and its sub-committees should continue to work toward the most effective utilization of Thailand's resources and those provided by the United States to promote Thailand's development and security.

The Foreign Minister and the Secretary were in full agreement that continued economic and social progress is essential to the stability of Thailand. They reviewed Thailand's impressive economic and social progress and the Thai Government's plans to accelerate development, particularly Thailand's continuing determination fully to utilize its own resources in moving toward its development goals.

The Foreign Minister and the Secretary of State also discussed the desirability of an early conclusion of a treaty of friendship, commerce and navigation between the two countries which would bring into accord with current conditions the existing treaty of 1937.

PROCLAMATION OF THE REVOLUTIONARY GROUP

Whereas the presentation of news and opinions by some newspapers has had an inappropriate character, for example, on some occasions has affected the Crown, and on some occasions has promoted approval of Communism, or has been a Communist plot to disturb and undermine national security such as might gravely imperil the country and welfare of the people, and whereas such actions cannot be prevented or abated by the authorities acting under the provisions of the Press Act now in force, the Revolutionary Group finds it proper to amend the said law when a legislative assembly is established. For the present, however, to prevent the said actions, it is found proper to lay down certain rules.

The Head of the Revolutionary Group, therefore, issues an order as follows:

1. Whoever wishes to act as printer, publisher, editor, or owner of printed papers bearing the same title, issued or intended to be issued continually whether or not the interval of publication is fixed or whether or not the matter printed in successive issues is related, shall file an application for a license with the authorities on the forms provided, and may proceed only upon being licensed by the authorities.

In case of breach of this rule, the authorities shall attach and destroy such papers and attach the machine on which such papers were printed for such period as they may think appropriate but not longer than six months.

2. If any paper publishes matter of the following nature:

(1) any matter infringing upon His Majesty the King, or defamatory, libellous, or contemptuous of the Queen, royal heir, or regent;

(2) any matter defamatory or contemptuous of the nation or Thai people as a whole, or any matter capable of causing the respect and confidence of foreign countries in regard to Thailand, the Thai Government, or Thai people in general, to diminish;

(3) any matter ambiguously defamatory or contemptuous of the Thai Government, or any ministry, public body, or department of the government without stating clearly the fault and matter;

(4) any matter ambiguously showing that the government or ministry, public body, or department of the government has deteriorated, is bad, or has committed a damaging offence without showing in what matter and particular;

(5) any matter promoting approval of Communism, or apparently a Communist plot to disturb or undermine national security;

(6) any false matter of a nature tending to panic, worry, or frighten the people or matter tending to incite, or arouse disorder, or conflict with public order or morality, or prophecies concerning the fate of the nation which might upset the people;

(7) any matter using coarse language tending to lower national morals or culture;

(8) any official secrets;

The competent authorities shall have the power to give warnings or seize and destroy such paper, or order the revocation of the license of the printer, publisher, editor or owner of the paper.

3. Anyone whose license has been revoked under Clause 2, shall have the right to appeal such order of the authorities to the under-secretary of the Ministry of Interior

within 15 days of the date of its receipt. The decision of the under-secretary shall be final.

4. The provisions of Clause 1 shall not affect printers, publishers, editors and owners of papers licensed prior to the date of this Proclamation.

Effective immediately.

Published on the 27th October 2501.

FIELD MARSHAL SARIT THANARAT
Head of the Revolutionary Group

ABOUT THE AUTHOR

LOUIS LOMAX was born in Valdosta, Georgia. He began his professional career as an assistant professor of sociology at Georgia State College, Savannah. At the age of twenty-four he turned to writing. His articles have appeared in major national magazines and he is the author of three highly regarded books: *The Reluctant African* (which won the Saturday Review Annisfield-Wolf Award for 1960), *The Negro Revolt,* and *When the Word is Given,* a study of the Black Muslim movement. Mr. Lomax now lives in Los Angeles, California, where he conducts his own twice-weekly television program on station KTTV. Mr. Lomax is also one of the most sought-after lecturers in the United States.